Omnipotence and Other Theological Mistakes

Omnipotence
and Other
Theological Mistakes

Charles Hartshorne

State University of New York • Albany

Published by
State University of New York Press, Albany

© 1984 State University of New York

All rights reserved

Printed in the United States of America

No part of this book may be used or reproduced in any manner whatsoever without written permission except in the case of brief quotations embodied in critical articles and reviews.

For information, address State University of New York Press, State University Plaza, Albany, N.Y., 12246

Library of Congress Cataloging in Publication Data

Hartshorne, Charles, 1897–
  Omnipotence and other theological mistakes.

  Includes index.
  1. God. 2. Ethics. I. Title.
BT102.H362 1984   231   83–6588
ISBN 0–87395–770–9
ISBN 0–87395–771–7 (pbk.)

Some Expressions of the New Theological Perspective

We do not honor God by breaking down the human soul, connecting it with him only by a tie of slavish dependence. It is his glory that he creates beings like himself, free beings . . . that he confers on them the reality, not the show, of power.

William Ellery Channing (1788–1842)

The fact that God could create free beings over against himself is the cross which philosophy could not carry, but remained hanging from.

Kierkegaard (1813–1855)

I . . . cherish the most certain of all truths and the one that should come first: I am free; beyond my dependence I am independent; I am a dependent independence; I am a person responsible for myself who am my work, to God who has created me creator of myself . . .

What a terrifying marvel: man deliberates and God awaits his decision . . .

Suddenly, O surprise . . . I have been witness of a change in the bosom of the absolute permanence . . . God, who sees things change, changes also in beholding them, or else does not perceive that they change.

Jules Lequier (1814–1862)

Should we say that because the later God develops beyond the earlier there was a defect in the earlier? But it was no other defect than that which progress to the higher itself determines, and each earlier time stands in this relation to a later time. . . . In this respect the world never advances, because this is the ground of the whole progress, to will something transcending the present . . . and the perfection of God generally is not in reaching a limited maximum but in seeking an unlimited progress. In this progress, however, the whole God in each time is the maximum not only of all the present, but also of all the past; he alone can surpass himself, and does it continually.

Gustav Theodor Fechner (1801–1887)

The traditional doctrines of theology do not solve the painful problem of evil. The ordinary conception of the creation of the world and the Fall turns it all into a divine comedy, a play that God plays with himself. . . . The freedom through which the creature succumbs to evil has been given to it by God, in the last resort has been determined by God. . . . When in difficulties, positive theology falls back upon mystery and finds refuge in negative theology. But the mystery has already been over-rationalized. . . . Freedom is not determined by God.

Nicolas Berdyaev (1874–1948)

Appealing to his [Einstein's] way of expressing himself in theological terms, I said: If God had wanted to put everything into the world from the beginning, He would have created a universe without change, without organisms and evolution, and without man and man's experience of change. But He seems to have thought that a live universe with events unexpected even by Himself would be more interesting than a dead one.

Karl Popper (1902–)

Contents

Preface

THE OCCASION WHICH LED to the writing of this book was somewhat sudden and quite concrete. It was the near co-incidence of two conversations, each with an intelligent, educated lady, different in the two cases, who was troubled by what she felt were absurdities in the idea of God with which she was familiar. In this way I was made more aware than ever before of a large number of people (represented by these two) who, not trained but seriously interested philosophically and theologically, know little or nothing about some important but relatively recent changes in the philosophy of religion. The objections that the two, and many others like them, make to a traditional and still widely accepted form of theology (which I call "classical theism") have been felt also by a number of penetrating, technically trained philosophers and theologians, especially in the present century, and these writers—not all of them as famous as they should be—have been working out, with increasing clarity and competence, a revised form of theism which some call "process theology" and I call "neoclassical theism," applying this term especially to my own version of the doctrine. This book is an attempt to present and defend the revised idea of God as simply and forcefully as I can. It is not written primarily for trained philosophers or theologians, although, to be candid, I should be surprised and disappointed if they could not learn from it, especially if they want to be able to meet a widespread need in contemporary society.

Since philosophers as well as theologians disagree, and no consensus is in sight, what they can honestly offer lay persons is not a doctrine to be accepted on their authority, but a clarification of the options for reasonable belief and of the arguments for and against these options. The final decision has to be individual, by each person at his or her own peril. Multitudes of people today are told by newspapers, and popular magazines or books, about options in nonreligious matters, but they are told little or nothing about the options in religion. The accessibility of options for belief is part of what religious freedom ought to mean. The options should be made more generally accessible than has been the case in the past. In this book it is one option that is directly presented, but it is defended against one vastly more widely known and for this reason may furnish a new opportunity to a fairly large class of people.

I have learned from responses to my previous writings that lives can be changed by showing that some of the traditional problems of belief—for instance how to reconcile the power and goodness of God with the evils we encounter in life—are genuinely solved, or at least greatly allieviated, by the view presented in this book. In writing it I have tried to avoid needless technicalities and professional paraphernalia in order to communicate with a wider circle of readers.

This is a candid book. I am not a fundamentalist in religion, and I make this entirely clear. But I definitely believe in God, in divine love as the key to existence, in love for God as (ideally) the all-in-all of our motivation, and in love for fellow creatures as valuable and important, judged by the same principle of value-to-God as we should judge ourselves by. In other words I accept what Jesus said was "the Law and the Prophets," that is, the gist of religion. If that makes me religious I think I am as religious as anybody. But it does not cause me to look down upon pious Jews (and there are some Jews who like my ideas), or upon Unitarians (ditto), or members of many other religious groups.

I express thanks to Colleen Kieke, whose typing, equal to the best encountered in a long writing career, I have for some years been enjoying. A superb typist, what a blessing that is!

As usual, but more than ever, I have reason and readers will have reason to thank Dorothy C. Hartshorne for her editorial help in the making of this book, the rapid writing of which made this help all the more necessary. It is the only book that I have ever written (apart from fine details) in five weeks. The book that preceded it and the one that is to follow it required many years to compose. Qualitative differences accompanying this quantitative difference are for others to judge.

C. H.

Chapter 1
Six Common Mistakes about God

The Mistakes Briefly Presented

IN THIS SECTION I introduce, with a minimum of criticism or argument, six ideas about God which have been held by a great number of learned and brilliant philosophers and theologians through many centuries and in many religious traditions, but which I and many others, including some distinguished modern theologians and philosophers, have found quite unacceptable. In other words, what we attack is an old tradition, but we attack it standing within a somewhat newer tradition. In this newer tradition there is a partial appeal (with reservations) to still a third tradition which is old indeed, expressed in various sacred writings, including the Old and New Testaments of the Bible. For it is our contention that the "theological mistakes" in question give the word *God* a meaning which is not true to its import in sacred writings or in concrete religious piety. This result came about partly because theologians in medieval Europe and the Near East were somewhat learned in Greek philosophy and largely ignorant of any other philosophy. This happened in both Christianity and Islam, to a somewhat lesser extent in Judaism. In all three religions there was a development of mysticism, which was different still and in some ways partially corrective of the all-too-Greek form taken by the official theologies.

In section B, I develop at length my arguments against the six mistakes, which together form what I call classical theism (the one too strongly influenced by Greek philosophy as medieval scholars knew that philosophy) and in favor of what I sometimes call the new theism, sometimes process theology, sometimes neoclassical theism—which is my version of a general point of view that has had a good many proponents in recent times.

First Mistake: God Is Absolutely Perfect and Therefore Unchangeable. In Plato's *Republic* one finds the proposition: God, being perfect, cannot change (not for the better, since "perfect" means that there can be no better; not for the worse, since ability to change for the worse, to decay, degenerate, or become corrupt, is a weakness, an imperfection). The argument may seem cogent, but it is so only if two assumptions are valid: that it is possible to conceive of a meaning for "perfect" that excludes change in any and every respect and that we must conceive God as perfect in just *this* sense. Obviously the ordinary meanings of perfect do not entirely exclude change. Thus Wordsworth wrote of his wife that she was a "perfect woman," but he certainly did not mean that she was totally unchangeable. In many places in the Bible human beings are spoken of as perfect; again the entire exclusion of change cannot have been intended. Where in the Bible God is spoken of as perfect, the indications are that even here the exclusion of change in any and every respect was not implied. And where God is directly spoken of as strictly unchanging ("without shadow of turning"), there is still a possibility of ambiguity. God might be absolutely unchangeable in righteousness (which is what the context indicates is the intended meaning), but changeable in ways compatible with, neutral to, *or even required by,* this unswerving constancy in righteousness. Thus, God would be in no degree, however slight, alterable in the respect in question (the divine steadfastness in good will) and yet alterable, not necessarily in spite of, but even because of, this steadfastness. If the creatures behave according to God's will, God will appreciate this behavior; if not, God will have a different response, equally appropriate and expressive of the divine goodness.

The Biblical writers were not discussing Greek philosophical issues, and it is at our own peril that we interpret them as if they were discussing these, just as it is at our peril if we take them to be discussing various modern issues that had not arisen in ancient Palestine. It may even turn out on inquiry that perfection, if taken to imply an absolute maximum of value *in every conceivable respect,* does not make sense or is contradictory. In that case the argument of the *Republic* is an argument from an absurdity and proves nothing. Logicians have found that abstract definitions may seem harmless and yet be contradictory when their meanings are spelled out. Example, "the class of all classes." Similarly, "actuality of all possible values," to which no addition is possible, may have contradictory implications. If perfection cannot consistently mean this value maximum, then the Platonic argument is unsound. Nor was it necessarily Plato's last word on the subject. (See Chapter 2B.)

Second Mistake: Omnipotence. God, being defined as perfect in all respects must, it seems, be perfect in power; therefore, whatever happens is divinely made to happen. If I die of cancer this misfortune is God's doing. The question then becomes,, "Why has God done this to me?" Here everything depends on "perfect in power" or "omnipotent." And here, too, there are possible ambiguities, as we shall see.

Third Mistake: Omniscience. Since God is unchangeably perfect, whatever happens must be eternally known to God. Our tomorrow's deeds, not yet decided upon by us, are yet always or eternally present to God, for whom there is no open future. Otherwise (the argument goes), God would be "ignorant," imperfect in knowledge, waiting to observe what we may do. Hence, whatever freedom of decision we may have must be somehow reconciled with the alleged truth that our decisions bring about no additions to the divine life. Here perfect and unchanging knowledge, free from ignorance or increase, are the key terms. It can be shown that they are all seriously lacking in clarity, and that the theological tradition resolved the ambiguities in a question-begging way.

It is interesting that the idea of an unchangeable omniscience covering every detail of the world's history is not to be found definitely stated in ancient Greek philosophy (unless in Stoicism, which denied human freedom) and is rejected by Aristotle. It is not clearly affirmed in the Bible. It is inconspicuous in the philosophies of India, China, and Japan. Like the idea of omnipotence, it is largely an invention of Western thought of the Dark or Middle Ages. It still goes unchallenged in much current religious thought.

But many courageous and competent thinkers have rejected it, including Schelling and Whitehead.

Fourth Mistake: God's Unsympathetic Goodness. God's "love" for us does not, for classical theists, mean that God sympathizes with us, is rejoiced or made happy by our joy or good fortune or grieved by our sorrow or misery. Rather God's love is like the sun's way of doing good, which benefits the myriad forms of life on earth but receives no benefits from the good it produces. Nor does the sun lose anything by its activity (we now know that this is bad astronomy). Or, God's beneficial activity is like that of an over-flowing fountain that remains forever full no matter how much water comes from it, and without receiving any from outside. Thus it is not human love, even at its best, that was taken as the model for divine love but instead two inanimate phenomena of nature, fictitiously conceived at that. Bad physics and astronomy, rather than sound psychology, were the sources of the imagery.

In short, argument from an insufficiently analyzed notion of perfection and a preference for materialistic (and prescientific) rather than truly spiritual conceptions were for almost two thousand years dominant in Western theology.

Fifth Mistake: Immortality as a Career after Death. If our existence has any importance for God, or if God loves us, He-She will not—it was argued—allow death to turn us into mere corpses. Hence, many have concluded, a theist must believe that we survive death in some form, and that the myths of heaven and hell have some truth in them. Here the assumption is that a mere corpse on the one hand and on the other hand survival in a new mode of heavenly or hellish existence (in which our individual consciousnesses will have *new* experiences not enjoyed or suffered while on earth) are the only possibilities. There is, however, as we shall see, a third possibility, quite compatible with God's love for us.

It is notable that in most of the Old Testament, for instance in the sublime Book of Job, individual immortality is not even mentioned. To this day, religious Judaism is much more cautious about affirming, and it often denies, such immortality. In the New Testament Jesus says little that seems to bear on the subject, and according to at least one very distinguished theologian (Reinhold Niebuhr), even that little is not decisive in excluding the third possibility just mentioned.

Sixth Mistake: Revelation as Infallible. The idea of revelation is the idea of special knowledge of God, or of religious truth, possessed by some people and transmitted by them to others. In some form or other the idea is reasonable. In all other matters people differ in their degree of skill or insight. Why not in religion? In the various sciences we acknowledge some people as experts and regard their opinions as of more value than those of the rest of us. The notion that in religion there are no individuals whose insight is any clearer, deeper, or more authentic than anyone else's is not particularly plausible. In all countries and in all historical times there have been individuals to whom multitudes have looked for guidance in religion. Buddha, Lao Tse, Confucius, Moses, Zoroaster, Shankara, Jesus, Muhammed, Joseph Smith, and Mary Baker Eddy were such individuals. New examples are to be found within the lives of many of us. Pure democracy or sheer equalitarianism in religious matters is not to be expected of our human nature. Some distinction between leaders or founders and followers or disciples seems to be our destiny. But there is a question of degree, or of qualification. To what extent, or under what conditions, are some individuals, or perhaps is some unique individual, worthy of trust in religious matters? It is in the answer to this question that mistakes can be made. Only a few years ago such a mistake sent hundreds to death, partly at their own hands, at Jonestown in British Guiana.

In religions that think of God as a conscious, purposive being, the idea of revelation can take a special form. Not simply that some are abler, wiser, than others in religion, as individuals may be in a science or in politics, but that divine wisdom has selected and so controlled a certain individual or set of individuals as to make them transmitters of the very wisdom of God to humanity. Since God is infallible (can make no mistakes), if no limitations are admitted to this conception of revelation, the distinction between fallible human beings and the infallible God tends to disappear. And so we find letters to newspaper editors in which the writer claims that his or her quotation from the Bible supporting some political position has the backing of "God almighty." Thus the essential principle of democracy, that none of us is divinely wise, that we all may make mistakes, is compromised.

One defence of claims to revelation is the reported occurrence of miracles. The fact, however, is that in every religion miracles are claimed. Hence the mere claim is not enough to establish the validity of the revelation. Buddha is reported to have spoken as a newborn infant. Was Shotoku Taishi, ruler-saint of seventh century Japan, shown to be of superordinary status by the fact that his death brought forth "rain from a cloudless sky"? Unless one believes (or disbelieves) all such accounts, how does one know where to stop?

What Went Wrong in Classical Theism

Two Meanings of "God Is Perfect and Unchanging." The word 'perfect' literally means "completely made" or "finished." But God is conceived as the maker or creator of all; so what could have made God (whether or not the making was properly completed)? 'Perfect' seems a poor word to describe the divine reality.

To describe something as "not perfect" seems a criticism, it implies fault finding; worship excludes criticism and fault finding. God is to be "loved with all one's mind, heart, and soul." Such love seems to rule out the possibility of criticism. Suppose we accept this. Do we then have to admit that God cannot change? Clearly yes, insofar as change is for the worse and capacity for it objectionable, a *fault* or *weakness*. God then cannot change for the worse. The view I wish to defend admits this. But does every conceivable kind of change show a fault or weakness? Is there not change for the better? We praise people when they change in this fashion. All healthy growth is such change. We are delighted in growth in infants and children. Is there nothing to learn from this about how to conceive God?

It is easy to reply that, whereas the human offspring starts as a mere fertilized single cell and before that as an unfertilized one, God is surely not to be so conceived. However, no analogy between something human and the worshipful God is to be taken in simple-minded literalness. There still may be an analogy between growth as a wholly good form of change and the divine life. For it is arguable that even an infinite richness may be open to increase. The great logician Bertrand Russell expressed this opinion to me, although Russell was an atheist and had no interest in supporting my, or any, theology.

The traditional objection, already mentioned, to divine change was that if a being were already perfect, meaning that nothing better was possible, then change for the better must be impossible for the being. The unnoticed assumption here has been (for two thousand and more years) that it makes sense to think of a value so great or marvelous that it could in no sense whatever be excelled or surpassed. How do we know that this even makes sense? In my view it does not and is either a contradiction or mere nonsense.

Bishop Anselm sought to define God's perfection as "that than which nothing greater (or better) can be conceived." In other words, the divine worth is *in all respects* strictly unsurpassable, incapable of growth as well as of rivalry by another. The words are smoothly uttered; but do they convey a clear and consistent idea? Consider the phrase 'greatest possible number.' It, too, can be smoothly uttered, but does it say anything? It might be used to define infinity; but I am not aware of any mathematician who has thought this a good definition. There are in standard mathematics many infinities unequal to one another, but no highest infinity. "Infinite" was a favorite word among classical theists; but they cannot be said to have explored with due care its possible meanings. In any case "not finite" is a negation, and the significance of the negative depends on that of the positive which is negated. If being finite is in every sense a defect, something objectionable, then did not God in creating a world of finite things act objectionably? This seems to me to follow.

Do or do not finite things contribute something to the greatness of God? If so, then each such contribution is itself finite. Does this not mean that somehow finitude has a valid application to the divine life? Consider that, according to the tradition, God could have refrained from creating our world. Then whatever, if anything, this world contributes to the divine life would have been lacking. Moreover, if God could have created some other world instead of this one, God must actually lack what the other world would have contributed. If you reply that the world contributes nothing to the greatness of God, then I ask, What are we all doing, and why talk about "serving God," who, you say, gains nothing whatever from our existence?

The simple conclusion from the foregoing, and still other lines of reasoning, is that the traditional idea of divine perfection or infinity is hopelessly unclear or ambiguous and that persisting in that tradition is bound to cause increasing skepticism, confusion, and human suffering. It has long bred, and must evermore breed, atheism as a natural reaction.

It is only fair to the founders of our religious tradition to remember that their Greek philosophical teachers who inclined to think of deity as wholly unchanging also greatly exaggerated the lack of novelty in many nondivine things. The heavenly bodies were unborn and undying, and changed only by moving in circles; species were fixed forever; the Greek atomists or materialists thought that atoms changed only by altering their positions. Heraclitus, it is true, hinted at a far more basic role for change, and Plato partly followed him. Plato's World Soul, best interpreted as an aspect of God, was not purely eternal, but in its temporal dimension "a moving image of eternity." However, Aristotle, in his view of divinity at least, was more of an eternalist even than Plato, and medieval thought was influenced by Aristotle, also by Philo Judaeus and Plotinus, who likewise stressed the eternalistic side of Plato. Today science and philosophy recognize none of the absolute worldly fixities the Greeks assumed—not the stars, not the species, not the atoms. It more and more appears that creative becoming is no secondary, deficient form of reality compared to being, but is, as Bergson says, "reality itself." Mere being is only an abstraction. Then is there no permanence, does "everything change"? On the contrary (see later, under topic 5), past actualities are permanent. My childhood experiences will be changelessly there in reality, just as they occurred. Change is not finally analyzable as destruction, but only as creation of novelty. The old endures, the new is added.

There are two senses in which freedom from faults, defects, or objectional features, and perfection in *that* sense, may be applied theologically. The divine, to be worthy of worship, must excell any conceivable being other than itself; it must be unsurpassable *by another*, exalted beyond all possible rivals. Hence all may worship God as in principle forever superior to any other being. This exaltation beyond possible rivals applies to both of the two senses of perfection that I have in mind. There are two kinds (or norms) of excellence, which differ as follows. With one kind it makes sense to talk of an absolute excellence, unsurpassable not only by another being but also by the being itself. This is what the tradition had in mind; and there was in it an important half truth. The neglected other truth, however, is that an absolute best, unsurpassable not only by others but by the being itself, is conceivable only in certain *abstract* aspects of value or greatness, not in fully concrete value or greatness. And God, I hold, is no mere abstraction.

The abstract aspects of value capable of an absolute maximum are goodness and wisdom, or what ought to be meant by the infallibility, righteousness, or holiness of God (one attribute variously expressed). We should conceive the divine knowledge of the world and divine decision-making about it as forever incapable of rivalry and in its infallible rightness incapable of growth. God is not first more or less wicked or foolish (or, like the lower animals, amoral, unaware of ethical principles) and then righteous and wise, but is always beyond criticism in these abstract respects, always wholly wise and good in relating to the world. It is not in such attributes that God can grow. This is so because goodness and rightness are abstract, in a sense in which some values are not.

Put a man in prison. He is not thereby necessarily forced to entertain wrong beliefs, lose virtue, or make wrong decisions. What he is forced to lose is the aesthetic richness and variety of his impressions. He cannot in the same degree continue to enjoy the beauty of the world. Similarly, a person suffering as Job did is not a happy person, but is not necessarily less virtuous than before. We can go further: ethical goodness and infallibility in knowledge have an upper or absolute limit. Whatever the world may be, God can know without error or ignorance what that world is and can respond to it, taking fully into account the actual and potential values which it involves, and thus be wholly righteous. But if the world first lacks and then acquires new harmonies, new forms of aesthetic richness, then the beauty of the world as divinely known increases. God would be defective in aesthetic capacity were the divine enjoyment not to increase in such a case. Aesthetic value is the most concrete form of value. Everything can contribute to and increase it. *An absolute maximum of beauty is a meaningless idea.* Leibniz tried to define it. Who dares to say that he succeeded? Beauty is unity in variety of experiences. Absolute unity in absolute variety has no clear meaning. Either God lacks any aesthetic sense and then we surpass God in that respect, or there is no upper limit to the divine enjoyment of the beauty of the world.

Plato viewed God as the divine artist, Charles Peirce and A. N. Whitehead termed God the poet of the world. Is the artist not to enjoy the divine work of art, the poet not to enjoy the divine poem? The Hindus attributed bliss to the supreme reality, and many Western theologians have spoken of the divine happiness, but a careful inquiry into the possibility of an absolute upper limit of happiness has not commonly been undertaken. Plato did write about "absolute beauty" but failed to give even a slightly convincing reason for thinking that the phrase has a coherent meaning.

It is not a defect of a Mozart symphony that it lacks the precise form of beauty which a Bach composition has. Aesthetic limitations are not mere defects. The most concrete form of value has no upper limit; there can always be additional values. God can enjoy all the beauty of the actual world and its predecessors, but creativity is inexhaustible and no actual creation can render further creation superfluous. Absolute beauty is a will-o-the-wisp, the search for which has misled multitudes. This is the very rationale of becoming, the reason why mere static being is not enough. Any actual being is less than there could be. There could be more, let there be more. To suppose that this has no application to God is to throw away such clues to value as we have, turn out the light, and use mere words to try to illuminate the darkness that is left.

Two Meanings of "All-Powerful." The idea of omnipotence in the sense to be criticized came about as follows: to be God, that is, worthy of worship, God must in power excel all others (and be open to criticism by none). The highest conceivable form of power must be the divine power. So far so good. Next question: what is the highest conceivable form of power? This question was scarcely put seriously at all, the answer was felt to be so obvious: it must be the power to determine every detail of what happens in the world. Not, notice, to significantly influence the happenings; no, rather to strictly determine, decide, their every detail. Hence it is that people still today ask, when catastrophe strikes, Why did God do this to me? What mysterious divine reason could there be? Why me? I charge theologians with responsibility for this improper and really absurd question.

Without telling themselves so, the founders of the theological tradition were accepting and applying to deity the *tyrant* ideal of power. "I decide and determine everything, you (and your friends and enemies) merely do what I determine you (and them) to do. Your decision is simply mine for you. You only think you decide: in reality the decision is mine."

Since the theologians were bright people we must not oversimplify. They half-realized they were in trouble. Like many a politician, they indulged in double-talk to hide their mistake even from themselves. They knew they had to define sin as freely deciding to do evil or the lesser good, and as disobeying the will of God. How could one disobey an omnipotent will? There were two devices. One was to say that God does not decide to bring about a sinful act; rather, God decides not to prevent it. God "permits" sin to take place. Taking advantage of this decision, the sinner does his deed. Yet stop! Remember that God is supposed to decide *exactly* what happens in the world. If someone murders me, God has decided there shall be precisely that murderous action. So it turns out that "permits" has here a meaning it ordinarily does not have. Ordinarily, when X gives Y permission to do such and such, there are at least details in the actual doing that are not specified by X (and could not be specified, since human language can give only outlines, not full details, of concrete occurrences). But omnipotence is defined as power to absolutely determine what happens. I have Thomas Aquinas especially in mind here. God gives a creature permission to perform act A, where A is no mere outline but is the act itself in its full concreteness. So nothing at all is left for the creature to decide? What then is left of creaturely freedom?

The most famous of all the scholastics finds the answer, and this is the second of the two devices referred to above. God decides that the creature shall perform act A, but the divine decision is that nevertheless the act shall be performed "freely." Don't laugh, the saintly theologian is serious. Serious, but engaging in double-talk. It is determined exactly what the creature will do, but determined that he or she will do it freely. As the gangsters sometimes say, after specifying what is to be done, "You are going to like it"—in other words, to do it with a will. If this is not the despot's ideal of power, what is?

What, let us ask again, is the highest conceivable form of power? Is it the despot's, magnified to infinity, and by hook or crook somehow reconciled with "benevolence," also magnified to infinity? This seems to have been the (partly unconscious) decision of theologians. Is there no better way? Of course there is.

After all, the New Testament analogy—found also in Greek religions—for deity is the parental role, except that in those days of unchallenged male chauvinism it had to be the father role. What is the ideal parental role? Is it that every detail is to be decided by the parent? The question answers itself. The ideal is that the child shall more and more decide its own behavior as its intelligence grows. Wise parents do not try to determine everything, even for the infant, must less for the half-matured or fully matured offspring. Those who do not understand this, and their victims, are among the ones who write agonized letters to Ann Landers. In trying to conceive God, are we to forget everything we know about values? To read some philosophers or theologians it almost seems so.

If the parent does not decide everything, there will be some risk of conflict and frustration in the result. The children are not infallibly wise and good. And indeed, as we shall argue later, even divine wisdom cannot completely foresee (or timelessly know) what others will decide. Life simply is a process of decision making, which means that risk is inherent in life itself. Not even God could make it otherwise. *A world without risks is not conceivable.* At best it would be a totally dead world, with neither good nor evil.

Is it the highest ideal of power to rule over puppets who are permitted to think they make decisions but who are really made by another to do exactly what they do? For twenty centuries we have had theologians who seem to say yes to this question.

Some theologians have said that, while God *could* determine everything, yet out of appreciation for the value of having free creatures, God chooses to create human beings to whom a certain freedom is granted. When things go badly, it is because these special creatures make ill use of the freedom granted them. As a solution of the problem of evil, this is perhaps better than the nothing that theorists of religion have mostly given us. But it is not good enough. Many ills cannot plausibly be attributed to *human* freedom. Diseases no doubt are made worse and more frequent by people's not taking care of themsleves, not exercising due care in handling food, and so forth. But surely they are not caused only by such misdoings. Human freedom does not cause all the suffering that animals undergo, partly from hunger, partly from wounds inflicted by sexual rivals or predators, also from diseases, parasites, and other causes not controlled by human beings.

There is only one solution of the problem of evil "worth writing home about." It uses the idea of freedom, but generalizes it. Why suppose that only people make decisions? People are much more conscious of the process of decision making than the other animals need be supposed to be; but when it comes to that, how conscious is an infant in determining its activities? If chimpanzees have no freedom, how much freedom has an infant, which by every test that seems applicable is much less intelligent than an adult chimpanzee? (One would never guess this fact from what "pro-lifers" say about a fetus being without qualification a person, so loose is their criterion for personality.)

There are many lines of reasoning that support the conclusion to which theology has been tending for about a century now, which is that our having at least some freedom is not an absolute exception to an otherwise total lack of freedom in nature, but a special, intensified, magnified form of a *general principle* pervasive of reality, down to the very atoms and still farther. Current physics does not contradict this, as many physicists admit. When will the general culture at least begin to see the theological bearings of this fact?

In philosophy of religion there is news, but newspapers know nothing of this. Nay more, periodicals of general interest know nothing of it. We have a population that inclines, in the majority, to be religious, but that shies away from any attempt at rational discussion of religious issues. This is an example of leveling down, rather than leveling up, democracy. People keep implying philosophical doctrines (why has God done this to me?) which philosophy of religion has largely outgrown, as also have the theologies which make some effort to be literate in philosophy and science.

Those who stand deep in the classical tradition are likely to object to the new theology that it fails to acknowledge "the sovereignty of God." To them we may reply, "Are we to worship the Heavenly Father of Jesus (or the Holy Merciful One of the Psalmist or Isaiah),or to worship a heavenly king, that is, a cosmic despot?" These are incompatible ideals; candid thinkers should choose and not pretend to be faithful to both. As Whitehead said, "They gave unto God the properties that belonged unto Caesar." Our diminished awe of kings and emperors makes it easier for us than for our ancestors to look elsewhere for our model of the divine nature. "Divine sovereignty" sounds to some of us like a confession, an admission that it is sheer power, not unstinted love that one most admires.

From childhood I learned to worship divine love. God's power simply is the appeal of unsurpassable love. Again Whitehead put it well: "God's power is the worship he inspires." It is not that we hear Zeus's fearful thunderbolt, see the lightning, and fall down at the sight of such power. No, we feel the divine beauty and majesty, and cannot but respond accordingly. Even the other animals feel it; what they cannot, and we can, do is to think it. Whitehead again: God leads the world by the "majesty" of the divine vision of each creature and its place in the world. God "shares with each actual entity its actual (past) world." "God is the fellow sufferer who understands."

Whitehead read in Plato and Aristotle the wonderfully enlightened doctrine that it is the divine beauty that moves the world. And what is the divine beauty, beyond all other beauties? A thousand voices, alas not quite audible in ancient Greece, have said it; but we still scarcely believe, much less understand, these voices: the beauty beyond all others is the beauty of love, that with which life has a meaning, without which it does not. The Greeks, however, had an argument, a subtly fallacious one, for denying that love is the ultimate principle. Love implies, they saw, that one fails to have in oneself all possible value and hence looks to another for additional value. Overlooked was the question-begging assumption that it even makes sense to "have in oneself all possible value," as though value is something that *could* be exhaustively actualized in one being all by itself. Were that possible, of course its possessor would not need another to love but would exist in solitary glory, incapable of enhancement in any way. And thus the one clue we have to life's meaning is cast away in favor of a merely verbal ideal of the exhaustive realization of possible good.

The novelist and playwright Thornton Wilder ends his novel *The Bridge of San Luis Rey* with the statement, "Love is the only meaning." In a later work, the play *The Alcestiad,* Wilder says, "Love is not the meaning. It is the sign that there is a meaning." In context both statements are valid. The love which, in the play, is not the meaning is the love of one human individual for another of the opposite sex. Certainly this is not *the* meaning, and certainly also it is, or can be, a sign that there is a meaning beyond the love in question. But a meaning beyond all love, human or otherwise— that is a will-o-the-wisp. Higher than one form of love is only a superior form. Grasp of this truth can be found in Ancient Egypt (Ikhnaton), India, China, and Palestine. In Ancient Greece it was not quite seen, and in Medieval Europe there was confusion between the Greek worship of mere eternity or mere "perfection" and the Palestinian worship of unstinted love.

Since any possible world, other than an utterly dead one (if that even makes sense, and some of us doubt it), must involve a multiplicity of individuals each making its own decisions, it follows (though for two thousand years it was not considered proper to say so) that there is an aspect of real *chance* in what happens. Aristotle and Epicurus knew this, and Plato implied it. But classical theism, supported by the Stoics among the Greeks, held that chance is merely a word for our ignorance of the ways of God. And classical science, until a few generations ago, inclined to hold that even apart from God, whatever happens is determined to happen by the situation in which it happens. The past, whether with or without God but including the laws of nature, determines what happens. The past, with or without God, is omnipotent, or has all-determining power. Our notion of deciding is illusory; heredity and environment decide for us. The psychologist Skinner says so. He may or may not believe in God; what is clear is that he does not believe in freedom, except so far as merely doing what we "like" to do constitutes freedom.

Byron wrote, as last line to his "Sonnet on Chillon," "For they appeal from tyranny to God." But how is it if God is the supreme, however benevolent, tyrant? Can we worship a God so devoid of generosity as to deny us a share, however humble, in determining the details of the world, as minor participants in the creative process that is reality?

To fully clarify our case against "omnipotence" we must show how the idea of freedom implies chance. Agent X decides to perform act A, agent Y independently decides to perform act B. So far as both succeed, what happens is the combination AB. Did X decide that AB should happen? No. Did Y decide the combination? No. Did any agent decide it? No. Did God, as supreme agent, decide it? No, unless "decide" stands for sheer illusion in at least one of its applications to God and the creatures. The word 'chance,' meaning "not decided by any agent, and not fully determined by the past," is the implication of the genuine idea of free or creative decision making—'creative' meaning, adding to the definiteness of the world, settling something previously unsettled, partly undefined or indeterminate. The combination AB, in the case supposed, was not made to happen by any intention of a single agent but by the chance combination of two intentions. Nor was it made to happen by the past; this is the idea of causal laws that physics is getting rid of and that some philosophers long ago gave good reasons for rejecting.

The new idea is that causal order is not absolute but statistical. It admits an element of chance or randomness in nature. Many of the leading physicists of recent times are quite explicit about this. But they were preceded in principle by some great Greek philosophers, some French philosophers of modern times, and the three most distinguished of purely American philosophers, Charles Peirce, William James and John Dewey. All events are "caused," if that means that they had necessary conditions in the past, conditions without which they could not have happened, however, what is technically termed "sufficient condition," that which fully determines what happens, requires qualification. Where there is little freedom, as an inanimate nature, there are often conditions sufficient to determine approximately what happens, and for most purposes this is all we need to consider. Where there is much freedom, as in the behavior of higher, including human, animals, there are still necessary conditions in the past, but sufficient past conditions only for a considerable range of possibilities within which each decision maker finally determines what precisely and concretely happens at the moment in the agent's own mind, that is, what decision is made. Even God, as the French Catholic philosopher Lequier said more than a century ago, waits to see what the individual decides. "Thou hast created me creator of myself." Many decades later Whitehead, also a believer in God, independently put the point with the phrase "the self-created creature"; and the atheist Sartre in France wrote of human consciousness as it own cause, *causa sui.*

Determinists claim that what makes us free is that our "character" as already formed, plus each new situation, determines our decisions. So then the child was determined by the character already formed in its infant past and by the surrounding world, and this character by the preceding fetus and world, and that by the fertilized egg? What kind of freedom is that? By what magic do people miss the fact they are misusing words? Skinner is right; once accept determinism and all talk of freedom is double-talk. The word 'voluntary' (liking it) is good enough for the determinist's freedom; why not stick to it, without trying to borrow the prestige of the glorious word 'freedom'? One's past character is *now* a mere fact, part of the settled world, almost like someone else's past character. One may be capable of creating a partly new and better character by using the genuine freedom, some of which one has already long had but perhaps has too little or too ill made use of.

Our rejection of omnipotence will be attacked by the charge, "So you dare to limit the power of God?" Not so, I impose no such limit if this means, as it seems to imply, that God's power fails to measure up to some genuine ideal. All I have said is that omnipotence as usually conceived is a false or indeed absurd ideal, which in truth *limits* God, denies to him any world worth talking about: a world of living, that is to say, significantly decision-making, agents. It is the *tradition* which did indeed terribly limit divine power, the power to foster creativity even in the least of the creatures.

No worse falsehood was ever perpetrated than the traditional concept of omnipotence. It is a piece of unconscious blasphemy, condemning God to a dead world, probably not distinguishable from no world at all.

The root of evil, suffering, misfortune, wickedness, is the same as the root of all good, joy, happiness, and that is freedom, decision making. If, by a combination of good management and good luck, X and Y harmonize in their decisions, the AB they bring about may be good and happy; if not, not. To attribute all good to good luck, or all to good management, is equally erroneous. Life is not and cannot be other than a mixture of the two. God's good management is the explanation of there being a cosmic order that limits the scope of freedom and hence of chance—limits, but does not reduce to zero. With too much freedom, with nothing like laws of nature (which, some of us believe, are divinely decided and sustained), there could be only meaningless chaos; with too little, there could be only such good as there may be in atoms and molecules by themselves, apart from all higher forms. With no creaturely freedom at all, there could not even be that, but at most God alone, making divine decisions—about what? It is the existence of many decision makers that produces everything, whether good or ill. It is the existence of God that makes it possible for the innumerable decisions to add up to a coherent and basically good world where opportunities justify the risks. Without freedom, no risks—and no opportunities.

Nothing essential in the foregoing is my sheer invention. I am summing up and making somewhat more explicit what a number of great writers have been trying to communicate for several centuries, or at least and especially during the last one hundred and fifty years.

The medieval doctrine of God's power was in fact virtually refuted i n its own time, by an Islamic scientist, philosopher, and poet Omar Khayyam, freely but—as an Arabic scholar has shown— essentially correctly translated by the superb English scholar-poet Edward Fitzgerald. As so often happens, the world did not fully grasp what had happened in the publication of his poem. It could be only a question of time until a new effort would have to be made to find a better way of interpreting the divine power.

We are . . .
But Helpless pieces of the Game He Plays
Upon this Checker-board of Nights and Days;
    Hither and thither moves, and checks, and slays,
And one by one back in the Closet lays. (Verse 69)

Oh Thou, who didst with pifall and with gin
Beset the Road I was to wander in,
    Thou wilt not with Predestined Evil round
Enmesh, and then impute my Fall to Sin. (Verse 80)

The theology Omar knew was Islamic; but Christianity at the time (eleventh century) was at best ambiguous on the issue of creaturely freedom that Omar was discussing. No theologian was ever more committed to the concept of omnipotence that I, like Omar, am criticizing than the Christian Jonathan Edwards. And he thought, with considerable justification, that he represented the tradition.

Of course Omar's comparison of a conscious animal with "pieces" in a game is nonsensical. But then so is the theology which supposes that such an animal can be entirely preprogrammed, or that its decisions can simply duplicate those made for it by another decision maker. Isaiah Berlin reports J. S. Austin as saying that while many talk about determinism, no one really believes it, "as we all believe that we shall die." This latter belief we take into account in our decision making (not enough, to be sure, but still we do take it into account). In contrast, it is impossible to take determinism into account, for it has no consistent practical meaning. *Before* I decide I may claim to know that my decision will be fully determined, whether by heredity and environment, or by God, but in what way can my decision take this alleged knowledge into account? *After* the decision I can say, See what I was preprogrammed to decide! But this in no way or degree helped me to make the decision. It was an idle retrospective application of a useless doctrine. The application in decision making is always too late.

The pieces on the chessboard are not decision makers, the reason being that they are not true singularities but crowds of singularities (molecules or the like). What such crowds "do" is shorthand for what its members do; *they* are the decision makers. And even classical physics over a century ago began to give up the attempt to conceive molecules as preprogrammed individually. Clerk Maxwell and C. S. Peirce took this to cast doubt on the deterministic idea, but they were geniuses; even after quantum theory there are those who still dream of a deterministic science. Einstein was perhaps the last genius to do this.

I feel that I ought to inform the reader, if he or she is not a philosopher, that today many philosophers defend the doctrine called "compatibilism," holding that determinism is compatible with human freedom. The reason they can do so is that they think of deciding merely as a psychological process of considering various ways of acting with the motives or reasons favoring or disfavoring the ways, and, without any sense of being constrained by anyone, adopting one of the ways. They do not seriously ask what objective significance the process has in the cosmos, what it does to the causal structure of the world. Moreover they are rather vague as to what the causal structure might really be.

Karl Popper says that when a physicist speaks of determinism he has a fairly precise idea of what he is talking about, but when a psychologist or philosopher talks about it "all precision vanishes." Peirce made similar charges. The causal structure of the world was in physics taken to be such that from the state of the whole universe (or an isolated system in it) in two successive moments all earlier and all later states follow exactly, given the natural laws really obtaining. Only ignorance of the previous successions of states and the laws would then explain our uncertainty about future states. But this is all talk about fairyland. We could not conceivably *not* be in partial ignorance, at least about previous states, if not also about the laws. Maxwell saw this over a century ago and remarked that since only God could possibly have the knowledge in question, and it is not the business of physics to discuss theological questions, determinism was not a proper doctrine of physics.

Maxwell probably did not know—few did in his time—that there are theologies which deny even to God knowledge of laws implying determinism, not because of divine limitations but because such laws describe no coherently conceivable world. They leave no room for genuine individuality, that is, for truly individual actions; and without individuals there are also no crowds or aggregates. To be is to act; to be individual is to act individually, that is, as not fully determined by another individual or set of individuals, past or eternal, according to strict law. From the universal to the fully individual there can be no deduction, no necessity. Laws are universals. If they have any role in reality it can only be to limit individual actions without fully determining them. They do forbid individuals to act in certain ways. This is true of many legal laws and moral principles. The principle of kindness does not tell us what in particular to do, but forbids whole classes of unkind actions. The "motives" that psychological determinism says determine actions are always more or less universal. We want to be "helpful" to someone we like, but no abstract idea like "helpful" can be as particular as what we actually do. Always finer decisions are left open by motives, ideals, or laws.

The idea of God fully determining, without constraining, our decisions can appeal to certain analogies. There is the hypnotic analogy. I take an actual case. The hypnotist says, "You will (later on) open the window." It is a cold day, the room is not in the least overwarm. You do open the window, giving some ingenious reasons for this. Has the hypnotist preprogrammed a particular piece of decision making? Not really. He has limited the options, at least as a matter of probabilities. (There is no proof that opening the window was *certain* to happen; there might have been a slight probability of its not happening.) But there are countless particular, subtly differing ways of opening a window. And those ingenious reasons for an odd action were not preprogrammed at all, so far as the data can prove. They were the real decisions, along with the exact timing, eact motions of the arm, and the like.

Again we can put pressure on people, or exert charm or more or less subtle suggestions, to get people to do what we want them, or think they ought, to do. But the actions themselves are always more particular than the wanting, or the idea of moral obligation.

There is no analogy that unambiguously supports determinism. It is a leap in the dark. No matter how brilliant a hypnotist, no matter how charming or subtly suggestive, God may be, the creature's concrete, fully definite decision has to be made by it, not by God. Whitehead's terminology is the most exact in history, by a good margin, to express the point. The creature must "prehend" God's "initial subjective aim" proposed to it. The proposed aim is in terms of universals called by Whitehead "eternal objects"—my own view does not eternalize universals to the extent Whitehead does—but the final subjective aim, which is the creature's fully particular decision, cannot follow or be uniquely specified by the initial subjective aim, which is really an outline, not an exact qualitative duplicate of the final aim.

Peirce, Bergson, and Whitehead realize, as may do not, that the ultimate freedom is not in "behavior" but in experience, just *how* that particular experience prehends its past, including in that past God's decision, already made, for the particular occasion. No matter what motives the past, including me as past, and other actualities offer me-now, I-now must still decide the precise concrete way in which I respond to this offering, just what relative prominence this or that factor receives in my experience of it. "The many become one and are increased by one." My past is a many of events or experiences, including my previous experiences; what is called my character as already formed is simply an aspect of the past history of experiences constituting a sequence of the type that used to be called one's stream of consciousness, the members of this stream having special prehensive relations to previous members and to that complicated society of societies of subhuman actualities making up what is called one's body. (More of this in Chapter 2.)

When determinists talk about freedom as action determined by one's own character, they are blurring together several factors which need distinguishing (illustrating Popper's lack of precision in nonphysicists). If the character in question is your or my *present* quality as experiencer, that and the present experience are simply two aspects of one actuality. Self-determination in that sense does not imply determinism; but, on the contrary, it means that my character as definite before the decision does not determine but only influences (via present prehension) the present character, decision, or experience.

The question of freedom as a merely psychological process, taken in abstraction from cosmology, is a rather trivial matter. The significance of freedom is in its role in the causal structure of the world. We face certain theoretical options. *Either* all that exists necessarily exists, *or* there is contingency. Spinoza and the Stoics explored the first option and it may well be left to them. (Few logicians see any merit in that way of viewing things.) If there is contingency, then *either* the transition from what could be to what is takes place by 'freedom', 'spontaneity', 'creativity', three words at least two of which are used by a number of thinkers (Bergson, Berdyaev, Peirce, and others), also 'decision' (Whitehead's favorite word here), *or* the transition does not take place by freedom but is just pure chance. It is, it might not be, *c'est tout.* This amounts to giving up any effort to throw light on contingency by any positive aspect of experience. Decision (on more or less conscious levels) we seem to experience. If chance or contingency are merely decision viewed from without or behavioristically, and as not fully determined by the past, we have explained a negation by something positive, which is pure gain as I see it.

Supposing that freedom or decision is the positive secret of contingency, that is, lack of necessity, we ask, "Whose freedom, who or what is the decision maker? Is it God, deciding for all?" Then, while God's decision is contingent, it might, it seems, leave no further contingency for any other being. All might in their supposed decisions necessarily duplicate their portions of the one Divine Decision. And then natural laws might, it seems, be more than approximate or merely statistical. For centuries thinkers leaned toward this theory more or less strongly. It was a bizarre idea. God, being supremely free, decides to have creatures not in the least free so far as this means resolving open options. For the One Decision has closed them, once for all, in eternity. Bizarre, bizarre!

The remaining theoretical option is that God, being supremely free, decides for creatures that are less than supremely, but still somewhat, free. Thus no unqualified determinism. By this sacrifice (what really is lost by it?) we gain—I am tempted to say—*everything.* A "world" now means an ordered, but not absolutely ordered, system of decision makers, whose decisions will have some chance aspects, with their mixtures of risks and opportunities. A world, any world, will be exciting, since in it agents really decide things every moment that previously (or from any purely eternal standpoint) were not decided. In any world, at every moment, even God encounters novelties, so that 'becoming' (in total abstraction from which no being can be anything but an empty cipher) applies even to God. In such a world there will be conflicts and frustrations. There is no longer the classical problem of evil. The question now is only, Is there not too much freedom, too great risk of evil, to be justified by the opportunities also open to the freedom? Thus the question becomes one of degree, and then the ancient defence, we are not wise like God and probably not in a position to second-guess divine decisions, becomes at least far stronger than it could be under the old idea of all-determining power (dealing only with the powerless). And at least we are no longer living in fairyland. We can recognize our world as a specimen of what has been abstractly described.

An interesting special case of the omnipotence problem is Abraham Lincoln's thought about it during the Civil War. "The will of God prevails," he said, and derived from this, though with some hesitation, that the war would last exactly as long as God willed it to last, since God, by "working in quiet" on the minds of men could determine it to end at any time. It is not clear just how far Lincoln went toward absolute theological determinism. Perhaps he thought that God made definite decisions only about fairly large-scale matters like the ending of a war. He suggested that a long war might mean God's will that the monstrous crime of slavery should be adequately punished. Yet "God's purposes are not our purposes." Lincoln also speaks about "the attributes we attribute to God," presumably referring especially to power and goodness. Like many theologians he seems somewhat more willing to confess our possible ignorance of God's goodness than of his power. Or is he about equally modest in both respects? Surely, unless we are to worship power more than goodness, it is at least as important that we should have a meaning applicable to God for 'goodness' as for 'power'; and what does "God is good" mean if the kind of purpose it implies is hopelessly opaque to us?

What use could Lincoln really be making of his view that God would determine the exact length of the war? How would it illuminate his own actions? Consider, too, that at the end of the war some Northerners would be much concerned to see to it that the South suffered as its rebellion made it "deserve" to suffer. If a long war occurred in order, in the divine judgment, to adequately punish the South (or the South and the North), this would not tell Northerners anything about what to do to prolong or shorten the war. For, only after the end came could one know what God willed in the matter. And if, after the end, one concluded that God had evidently willed the South's suffering to end, this would really be illogical, since other ways to make the South suffer than in war would be quite possible. So Lincoln's forgiveness of the South might be against the will of God? Ah, but wait and see! The will of God prevails. Then was the assassination divinely willed so that the punishment of the South could continue? Where do we stop in this second-guessing of God?

The only livable doctrine of divine power is that it influences all that happens but determines nothing in its concrete particularity. "Knowing" afterwards exactly what God has willed to happen is useless. We can, I believe, know the *general principle* of God's purpose. It is the beauty of the world (or the harmonious happiness of the creatures), a beauty of which every creature enjoys its own glimpses and to which it makes its unique contributions, but each created stage of which only God enjoys adequately, everlastingly, and as a whole, once it has been created.

Lincoln was a noble soul, supremely great, and he made no bad use of the theology he knew. But he could perhaps have gained something from a better theology. Still more could many souls, less wise and strong, gain what they sorely lack if they were spared useless riddles about divine power and could focus on the inspiration of seeing life as, even in its least moments, permanent contributions to the stores of beauty available selectively and partially to future moments and inclusively and fully to God. Also of believing in God as ideally powerful—in whatever sense this is compatible with having free creatures whose satisfactions and dissatisfactions are divinely participated in—God, who can hurt no one without vicariously suffering Him-Her-self, and can gratify no one without vicariously enjoying this gratification. So God's purpose is the welfare of the creatures as the means, finally, to increase the divine happiness, whose value is no absolute maximum but an ever-enriched infinity.

As a final verbal clarification, I remark that if by 'all-powerful' we mean that God has the highest conceivable form of power and that this power extends to all things—not as, with us, being confined to a tiny corner of the cosmos—and if this is what the word 'omnipotent' can be understood to mean, then yes, God is omnipotent. But the word has been so fearfully misdefined, and has so catastrophically misled so many thinkers, that I incline to say that the word itself had better be dropped. God has power uniquely excellent in quality and scope, in no respect inferior to any coherently conceivable power. In power, as in all properties, God is exalted beyond legitimate criticism or fault finding. In this power I believe. But it is not power to have totally unfree or "absolutely controlled" creatures. For that is nonsense.

Two Meanings of "All-Knowing." The word 'omniscient' seems somewhat less badly tarnished by its historical usage than 'omnipotent.' Whereas having all power (of decision making) would be a monopoly, implying that the creatures had no such power, having all knowledge has no monopolistic implications. Only one agent can genuinely make a certain concrete decision; in contrast, many agents can know one and the same truth, e.g., that two and three is five, or that Julius Caesar was assassinated by Brutus. Hence that God knows all truth is quite compatible with you or your brother knowing many truths.

With omniscience there is one difficulty: either knowing about the future differs essentially from knowing about the past, and hence even God knows our past decisions in one way and knows about the future of our decision making in another way, or else it is merely our human weakness that for us the future is partly indefinite, a matter of what may or may not be, whereas God, exalted altogether beyond such a "limitation," sees the future as completely definite. If God is to be thought in every respect immutable it is this second option that must be taken; but have we any other reason for rejecting the old Socinian proposition that even the highest conceivable form of knowledge is of the past-and-definite *as* past-and-definite and of the future and partly indefinite *as* future and partly indefinite? Otherwise would not God be "knowing" the future as what it is not, that is, knowing falsely? As we have seen, the arguments for the complete unchangeability of God are fallacious; hence, the arguments for growth in God's knowledge, as the creative process produces new realities to know, are sound. Thus as Fechner, Berdyaev, Tillich, and, probably independently, Whitehead held (and Berdyaev most neatly formulated), our existence from moment to moment "enriches the divine life." And this is the ultimate meaning of our existence.

Is God all-knowing? Yes, in the Socinian sense. Never has a great intellectual discovery passed with less notice by the world than the Socinian discovery of the proper meaning of omniscience. To this day works of reference fail to tell us about this.

God's Love as Divine Sympathy, Feeling of Others' Feelings. Throughout the Christian centuries there have been a few theologians who have rejected the conception of God as pure intellect or will, as knowing our feelings but feeling nothing, willing our good but not in any intelligible sense *caring* about our pleasures or sufferings. Most theologians rejected feeling as a divine attribute. For them it connoted weakness. True, the Church father Origen said that God felt compassion for humanity and therefore sent the Son as Redeemer. But Origen did not systematically develop the point into a significant philosophical doctrine. In general God was not thought of as sharing our griefs and joys. It was not clear at all that the divine knowledge of our feelings was itself feeling. Fechner, the nineteenth-century psychologist, was perhaps the first great exception to this tradition. The nonconformist English theologian A. E. Garvie was a more recent one. He wrote of the "omnipatience" of God, meaning the divine sympathy with our experiences.

The honor of presenting a worked-out technical philosophical system in which the idea of divine sympathy has its natural place goes to Whitehead, with Fechner the principal anticipator. According to Whitehead, the basic relationship in reality is "prehension," which in the most concrete form (called "physical prehension") is defined as "feeling of feeling," meaning the manner in which one subject feels the feelings of one or more other subjects. In other words, 'sympathy' in the most literal sense. And Whitehead used this word also. Moreover, God is said to know the world by physical prehensions, in other words by feeling the feelings of all the subjects composing that world.

In this philosophy it is not mere benevolence that constitutes the divine nature, it is love in the proper sense. Cruelty to other creatures, or to oneself, means contributing to vicarious divine suffering. Hence, of *course* we should love our fellows as we love ourselves, for the final significance of their joy or sorrow is the same as the final significance of our joy or sorrow, that they will be felt by God. Just so did Fechner see the matter. But the world paid no attention, as it had paid no attention to the Socinian idea of divine knowledge. Merely being right is not enough to impress the busy world, always wrapped up in its more or less unconscious preconceptions. To Whitehead some attention has been paid, but how little compared to the fuss made about Einstein! As Whitehead once remarked to me, Einstein had "all the marks of a great man." Nevertheless, the reason for his fame was not merely the greatness of his discoveries. It was also the fact that they had applications to our physical manipulations of nature, vast industrial and military implications. Theological discoveries are less obvious in their importance.

In fairness to the classical theologians, one thing needs to be said. They realized, quite rightly, that in thinking about God we are likely to apply to deity adjectives that are appropriate enough when applied to ourselves but are unworthy of application to the being exalted above all others, actual or conceivable, and because of this exalted status worthy of being worshiped. To use the word generally employed here, we must in theology beware of *anthropomorphism*, reading our own human traits into our portrait of deity. When theologians read about Jehovah being "angry," they said, "Surely God is above such emotions as anger, along with those of envy, jealousy, and the like!" All these indications of human weakness in the Biblical account of deity were set aside as concessions to the ignorance or innocence of ordinary people, incapable of the refinements of scholarship or philosophy. Human beings are theologically said to be "images of God"; but the danger of underestimating the vast difference between creatures and Creator is obvious. What seems so strange in the traditional, largely Greek, conception of God adopted in the Dark Ages and kept intact through the Middle Ages and beyond is partly explained by the vigorous and—if kept within its proper limits—justified effort to keep clear of anthropomorphic tarnishing of the description of God. Certainly, a being totally and in every respect immmutable and open to no increase in value is extremely different from ourselves; however, it is far from clear that anything is left of the "image of God" that is supposed to be in us, and that indeed must be in us if we are to have any idea of God.

What it comes to is that in retreating from popular anthropomorphism classical theology fell backward into an opposite error. Intent on not exaggerating the likeness of the divine and the human, they did away with it altogether, if one takes their statements literally. Using the word 'love', they emptied if of its most essential kernel, the element of sympathy, of the feeling of others' feelings. It became mere beneficience, totally unmoved (to use their own word) by the sufferings or joys of the creatures. Who wants a friend who loves only in that sense? A heartless benefit machine is less than a friend.

If anyone has been more learned in medieval thought than the Jewish scholar Harry Wolfson I have not learned his name. Wolfson's considered judgment was that the scholastic theology utterly failed to express the Biblical idea of God. Many Christian scholars, including the father of the author of this book, have agreed with Wolfson. Many more-or-less skeptical or agnostic philosophers have also agreed with the judgment. A well-meaning attempt to purify theology of anthropomorphism purified it of any genuine, consistent meaning at all. After all, the problem of anthropomorphism is not so simple that only one kind of mistake can be made in dealing with it. If an anthropomorphic idea is one that expresses our human nature, in what sense can we have a nonanthropomorphic idea? Said Emerson, "All of the thoughts of a turtle are turtle." Is it any less true that all of a human being's thoughts are human?

Human beings, unlike turtles, have not only ideas but ideas about ideas. We can make of abstractions things to talk about. If our ideas are all human, we are the ones who can say that this is so. Can the turtle say or in any way think the corresponding thought about itself? Probably not. What is the moral? Charles Peirce

discussed the matter and came to the conclusion that human thought
has no alternative to thinking in terms of partial analogies between
human nature and nonhuman things.

Consider: a physicist formulates a system of concepts, mathe-
matically definite, and observes nature to see if there is a corre-
spondence between this system and predictable results of experi-
ments. He is testing an analogy between his *thinking* and what goes
on in nature. What the physicist does *not* do is to even consider
the possibility of any analogy, close or remote, between his *emotions*
and what goes on in nature. This does not prove that there are
nothing like emotions in nature. At most it proves only that for
the purpose of predicting observable, measurable changes in inanimate parts of nature, consideration of how things may or may
not feel is superfluous or unhelpful.

In biology, and above all in psychology, however, the question
of nonhuman emotions is bound to arise. Only the future will tell
how far down the scale of animals toward one-celled organisms
and perhaps farther the question can be pursued with scientifically
significant results. At present only some philosophers and a few
scientists in unofficial moments are paying much attention to the
question. What this proves is at most only that the time is not yet
ripe for a determined assault on the problem. It is a postponed
topic on the agenda. (More of this in the next chapter.)

Among nonhuman things to be dealt with by thought that itself
remains human, there are many gradations of difference from our
human nature. The difference admits two opposite extremes. There
is the extremely subhuman: how does an atom, a particle (or
"wavicle"), differ from a human being? Obviously the difference
is so vast as to stagger the imagination. At the opposite extreme,
how does the uttermost form of the superhuman, the divine, differ
from a human being? Here too the analogy seems extended to the
breaking point. Indeed the difference is here incomparably greater.
For deity is not merely vastly different from ourselves, the difference
is more than quantitative or a difference of degree. God alone is
conceived as unborn and undying, without possible beginning or
termination of existence. Classical theists were impressed, and rightly
so, by the radical nature of this distinction from all ordinary things.
Yet they forgot that human thinking, even about God, cannot cut

its human root. They made God, not an exalted being, but an empty absurdity, a love which is simply not love, a purpose which is no purpose, a will which is no will, a knowledge which is no knowledge. We are forced to make a new beginning, unprecedented except for a few exceptional and neglected figures, Socinus, Fechner, and some others.

Once more let us try to be fair. The theologians I am criticizing knew that they were skating on thin ice. So they skated warily around what seemed the thinnest places. Thus they said, "We know only what God is not, we do not know what God is positively." But of course they had to retreat now and then from complete consistency with this merely negative position. Between good and bad they said that God is good. This goodness had to be something humanly intelligible to some degree. Otherwise why worship God? As F. H. Bradley sarcastically suggested we cannot worship the Unknowable on the ground that "we do not know what the devil it may be." *Being* too was attributed to God, with some such proviso as "being itself," or *ens a se,* self-sufficient being, self-existing being. Also God was regarded as *causing or creating* the world, so creative action was positively asserted.

Moreover, it is not correct to regard negative statements as necessarily more modest or safe than positive ones. To assert that that is no change in any respect or of any kind in God—as it were, to forbid God to change—is to imply: either there is no essentially good kind of change, the lack of which would be a defect, or else God suffers from this defect. Do we know that there is no essentially good kind of change, lack of which would be a defect? I say that we do not know this. If we know anything in these matters, we know that there is an essentially good kind of change, which is an increase in the aesthetic richness of one's knowledge, as the aesthetic richness of what exists to be known increases. And the idea of an absolute maximum of aesthetic richness is contradictory or meaningless. Hence no world that God knew could actualize for him all possible aesthetic value. The conclusion is that the alleged modesty of "the negative way" in theology was definitely overrated. It was a species of presumption after all.

Paul Tillich's assertion that all statements about God are merely "symbolic" is a variant of the negative way in theology. He does qualify it by saying that God is literally Being Itself. That this has a good meaning is easily seen from the consideration that if God infallibly knows all truth, then to be is to be-for-God (as known to Him-Her). But, alas, Tillich deduces from this that "God is not *a* being," an individual. Is God then a mere universal, an empty abstraction? Overlooked by Tillich is the consideration that, although 'a being' suggests one being among others like it, God's being an individual does not have to mean this. God can be, not simply *a* being, but *the* being, essential to all, strictly unique in status. For this being is universally relevant, the Subject to whom all individuals are infallibly known objects, and upon whom all individuals depend.

Two Meanings of "Immortality." One of the penalties of being the freely thinking animals that we are is that, whereas the other animals probably do not consciously know that they are fated to die, we do know it. If "All's well that ends well" is a sound principle, what are we to make of the apparent facts that a human life ends in death and that being dead seems as far as possible from being well? Confronted with this riddle, human beings everywhere have tended to tell themselves tall stories about what being dead is really like. Only the ancient Jews and some of the ancient Greeks were nearly free from this flight from what, for all we really know, is the human condition. In the sublime Book of Job, where the human destiny is reflected upon with great depth and nobility, there is not a word about survival of death. Job worships God, not because God will grant him bliss beyond the grave, but simply because God is worshipful, because worship is the appropriate response to the supreme Creative and Receptive Spirit of the cosmos. A rather different attitude is found in Dante's powerful, beautiful poem— splendid literature, but is it sound theology?

As usual, there are ambiguities in the statement of the problem. Life "ends in death" has more than one possible meaning. If "ends in" means "becomes nothing but," then the statement is an absurdity. A conscious state of life cannot *become* an unconscious state of being dead. Consciousness is consciousness, unconsciousness is unconsciousness, the one cannot *be* the other. When we write the biography of a person we are not describing a corpse or a heap of dust. We are describing a stream of experiences and bodily activities, of none of which a corpse is capable. Are we describing a mere nothing; is what we say of the deceased person's life not true; or if true what is it true of? What is the past anyway? It is almost beyond belief how little most philosophers have dealt with this question. What is history about if yesterday's or last year's or last century's events are now simply unreal? It is now that we try to speak truthfully about the past; there must be something to make our statements true if we succeed.

I had a rather happy childhood. Where and what is that child's happiness? I have only a few faint memories of it now. Surely they are not what make it true—if it is true—that I experienced thousands of happy hours, as well of course as some not so happy! Go to the town where I spent my childhood—you will not find my happy hours there. Yet they are not nothings, they are still definite realities, constituents of the total reality about which true statements can still be made.

If Julius Caesar is now nothing, then how could any statement about him be truer than any other? *Nothing* has no definite characteristics. Is history only about, not what *did* exist, but what still survives by way of documents, records, monuments? Most historians think history is about more than such relics. (I am quoting one of them.)

The structure of time can be conceived in a few basic ways among which we need to choose. We often speak as though only what "exists now" has any reality at all, and what merely did exist is simply nonexistent. Yet a little reflection shows us that apart from our knowledge of the past we know virtually nothing. What exists right now is what we have *not yet had time to know*. Sounds take seconds at least to reach our consciousness, and even sights are perceived only after an interval spanned by the speed of light. Conscious knowledge is of the past or nothing. Beware then of lightly dismissing the past as candidate for the status of reality! If it is unreal, what reality is there?

It happens that a few philosophers have reflected with care upon the status of the past. They include Bergson in France, the American Peirce, and the Anglo-American Whitehead. Peirce put it neatly: "The past is the sum of accomplished facts." Or again, "It is the past which is actual." If actuality is what acts upon us, relativity physics tells us that effective actions (apart at least from some extremely slight quantum influences) take time to pass from agent to patient. What is now happening elsewhere has yet to effectively influence us.

Whitehead has put the matter in terms of his doctrine of "the objective immortality of the past." Once an event has occurred it is a permanent item in reality. The "accomplished facts" that constitute the past cannot be de-accomplished or nullified. If they could, historical truth would be impossible or meaningless.

The permanence of the past in every subsequent present is made to some extent concrete by considering memory and perception. What we just felt or thought is still somehow there in our experience by immediate memory, which is different from recollection, that is, recalling to consciousness what for a time has been forgotten. Primary memory is having awareness of an experience before it has been dismissed from consciousness. Perception (at least of things at a distance), as already pointed out, relates us to the past, at most reaching the present with the speed of light. These are the human ways in which the past pervades the present. If these human forms of possessing the past are all that there are, then indeed is the past severely limited in reality.

At this point one of the advantages of believing in God becomes apparent. What in us is extemely partial, feeble retention of the past may in God be complete, ideally vivid and adequate retention. My happy childhood was a gift the world and my parents offered to God. God does not lose what God has once acquired. So what makes history true, if it is true, is the really preserved past as it is in God, who is the final "measure of all things," and not—in spite of Protagoras—our human mode of thinking and knowing. One of some six reasons I have for belief in God is that it makes intelligible, as nothing else does, how there can be historical truth.

Does life end in death? A book ends with its last sentence or last word; however, the book does not *become* the mere silence or blank page following that word. The book of life is all its "words" (actions, experiences), and these form an imperishable totality, as adequately retained in the divine life. A conscious life remains that forever, it can never be mere unconsciousess. But lives (other than God's), like books and works of art generally, have beginnings and endings, they are finite entities. Only so can they have definite form and distinctiveness. Those who want to go on being themselves forever and yet pass on to additional experiences after death are either asking for unbearable monotony, endless reiterations of the same personality traits, or they are asking for a unique prerogative of God, ability to achieve self-identity through no matter how great and diverse changes and novelties. Unconsciously they either want to be bored to death, so to speak, or to be God. This is the only way I can see the conventional idea of personal immmortality. I am not alone in this. Nevertheless, there must be a good meaning for immortality. *Death is not destruction of the reality we have achieved.* It is this reality's achievement of final definiteness, the full completion of it as gift to the world and the divine life. (The sense in which death is destructive in particular cases will be discussed later.)

If we now return to the argument, "God who loves us will not destroy us," we shall find several things wrong with this argument. First, it assumes that the past is unreal. Accordingly, what a person is *just before* death is all that death "destroys." In most cases this would be a rather insignificant loss. Indeed, if we are really beings with an infinite future before us, and in that sense like God, what does death amount to? From an infinite sequence of experiences death deprives us of a small finite number on this earth and substitutes a comparable addition in a perhaps better place. The traditional Western view of immortality, making us infinite in one respect and in that respect rivals of deity, really ruins any sensible perspective on human affairs.

Second, the argument seems to assume, falsely, that it is God who decides when and how we shall die. This, of course, involves the very idea of omnipotence, the absurdity of which has been shown earlier. When and how we die is decided by no single agent, but by innumerable creatures, including ourselves, other people, and countless subhuman agents, such as bacteria, molecules, and the cells of our own bodies, all interacting in partly chance fashion. There is no scapegoat, no single agent who decides the details of creaturely existence. Anthropology shows us clearly how inclined human beings are to find a scapegoat, someone to blame. What is it all but superstition and unwillingness to face reality?

If we are truly mortal animals, then our lives are finite in time as well as in space. What is indeed immortal (the reality of the past) is precisely this finite series of experiences and deeds. Death subtracts not an iota of the lives we have already enjoyed before the moment of death. What death does nullify are the not yet actualized possibilities of living. This can be a cause of grief, and, in the case of homicide, of blame. *Just because our careers are finite* the loss of many years of significant living can be tragic. Instead of a rounded career, such as many fortunate persons have enjoyed, there is a truncated half career, in which much that has been purposively prepared for can never be realized. We are animals who "look before and after"; we live in part for our earthly futures. To know that at any moment, either by chance or by malicious intention, our careers may come to an end, gives a tragic tinge to our existence.

What is the alternative? Is it that the world should be so absolutely controlled that there would be no chance of premature death? This implies that it makes sense to talk of absolutely controlled individual creatures. In terms of current metaphysics of process an individual is to some extent self-controlled or nothing. Is the alternative that we should be immortal, incapable of having our careers terminated? This means that we would, in one respect, our future, be as infinite as God is. Why then should we not, like God, be ubiquitous in space? It is not enough to say that we are "finite" spatially. We are mere fragments of the spatial whole. And that such fragmentary creatures should have temporally infinite futures is not an immediately reasonable proposition.

Consider now the idea that a loving God would not establish natural laws that make eventually dying a certainty for animals such as we are. God loves us, this I believe. But as what does God love us? I answer, God loves us as what we are, a certain very distinctive species of mortal animal, finite spatially and in careers. We are each divinely loved as rendered individual and definite by this finitude. Moreover, and here I agree with the German philosopher Heidegger and his admirers, it is precisely as finite in this sense that we should love ourselves and our human fellows. As such I have for fifty-four years loved a wife, as such I love a daughter, grandson, and granddaughter. I need no tall stories about a supernatural kind of animal to love these persons, and many others as well. Nor do I need such stories to love God as the all-surpassing form of love.

Of course the immortality of the past in God does not give people everything they may happen to want. Creatures indistinctly aware of God (even when they verbally call themselves atheists) are also aware of desires that the real world partially frustrates. We have been enjoying a spouse, a son or daughter, a friend, and our capacity for such enjoyment is not exhausted. So we may find it pleasant to think of continuing the relationship after death. However, if we know anything at all about the human condition it is that things do not always go as we might wish. Also we know that in this life the wicked are not always—if even usually—punished in proportion to their misdeeds, nor are the good rewarded in proportion to their good deeds. However, because of freedom in the creatures, without which they would not exist, an element of chance interaction is inevitable; it follows that some disappointments will occur. Nothing in all this appears a sufficient reason to demand a supernatural arrangement according to which, in some unimaginable way, and in spite of the freedom without which there could be neither evil nor good, the eventual satisfaction of all wishes will be guaranteed, or at least the full rewarding and punishment of all good and bad deeds. Freud, I must confess, seems to me to have given the bottom line concerning such an idea when he remarked, "The world is not a kindergarten." And indeed, even in the best-managed kindergarten some wishes are frustrated.

Revelation, "Infallible" as from God, "Fallible" as Humanly Received. It seems that there are persons who have better insight into religious truth than most of us do. The extreme way to put this is to say that while most of us guess and grope and wonder, these persons simply and absolutely know. If they write, their words impart absolute truth. The opposite extreme is to say that, in religious matters, no one knows any better than anyone else, that we are all equally at a loss (or else that only the atheists and skeptics are right). Between these extremes there are various gradations. In general it is rational to be suspicious of extremes. Indeed, in the five topics previously considered, I have been arguing for a view that mediates between extremes. Let us see this in some detail.

In topic number 1 the classical view was the extreme possible version of the assertion of absolute, unsurpassable, and unchangeable divine perfection. The opposite extreme is to deny that any being is strictly unsurpassable or unchangeable in any respect. The view defended was that there is indeed *unsurpassable, unchangeable divine perfection, but it is only an abstract aspect of deity, which concretely is self-surpassable yet not surpassable by others, and changeable only for the better.* And this view is defended on the ground that the idea of a value in every sense or by every valid criterion unsurpassable is either a contradiction or without any clear meaning.

In topic number 2, one extreme is the assertion of a highest conceivable creative and controlling power that is capable of monopolizing decision-making, of fully determining the details of the world, leaving no matters open for decision by the individuals constituting the world. At the opposite extreme is the denial that there is any highest conceivable or supreme form of power creative of and controlling the world, or the assertion that, given any power, a greater power is conceivable. The mediating position is that *there is a highest conceivable or supreme power, creative of and controlling the world,* but it does not and could not achieve the absurdity of monopolizing decision-making; rather, it is *creative of and controls individuals with some decision-making power of their own,* some ability to settle details left undetermined by the highest power. The argument is that only in this form is the highest power either consistently conceivable or worthy of worship.

In topic number 3, one extreme is the idea of a highest conceivable or divine knowledge, which correctly and changelessly surveys events throughout time and in this sense is free from error or ignorance. The opposite extreme is the denial that there is any highest conceivable form of knowledge, free from error or ignorance. The mediating position is that *there is a highest conceivable or divine knowledge, free from error or ignorance;* however, since events in time do not form a totality fixed once for all, but are an endlessly growing accumulation of additional actualities, to view all time in a changeless fashion would be an erroneous view and not at all the highest conceivable or divine form of knowledge. As the Socinians said, once for all, future events, events that have not yet happened, are not there to be known, and the claim to know them could only be false. *God does not already or eternally know what we do tomorrow, for, until we decide, there are no such entities as our tomorrow's decisions.* Jules Lequier in France, acquainted with the Socinians' doctrine, went over the problem with great care and came to the same conclusion they had. In Germany Fechner and the theologian Pfleiderer, probably independently, reached the same result. In Italy, England, and the United States, somewhat later, a number of thinkers dealt with the same set of problems, reaching similar conclusions.

In topic number 4, one extreme is the classical view that God, though said to be loving, is without anything like emotion, feeling, or sensitivity to the feelings of others and is wholly active *("actus purus,"* a fine example of a seemingly clear but yet absurd formula) rather than passive in relation to the creatures. Aristotle said it first: God is mover of all things, unmoved by any. At the opposite extreme is the polytheistic view found in Greek mythology whose superhuman beings, the gods, are capable of all sorts of emotional disturbances; they are jealous, easily offended, desirous sexually, and yet immortal. The mediating view is that God is *loving in the sense of feeling, with unique adequacy, the feelings of all others,* entirely free from inferior emotions (except as vicariously participated in or sympathetically objectified), *entirely steadfast in the constancy of the divine care for all, but, in response to the novelties in the creatures, with ever partly new experiences.* What never changes is the *adequacy* of the divine feelings of creaturely feelings; however, adequate response to a world lacking you or me, for example, would not be adequate response to a world with you or me. The contention is that only such a view can do justice to the biblical message at its best, and that, quite apart from the Bible, only such a view is really a coherent, intelligible way of conceiving God in terms of human experience, yet as in principle surpassing not only human nature but any conceivable animal nature, or any positively conceivable super-animal nature, other than God as so conceived.

The first four topics have concerned the nature of God, not in relation to the human species in particular, but in relation to creatures in general. Topics 5 and 6 introduce special relations between God and the human species.

In topic number 5 one extreme view is that after death a human career goes on forever in some supernatural realm; the other extreme view is that after death a human career is not only terminated but that the entire career, with all its joys and sorrows, all its actual beauty and richness, is reduced to nothing, as though it had never been. Of course no one consistently holds this, but innumerable people vaguely approach such a view in their minds and many a philosopher seems little wiser. The mediating view is that an entire career, with all its concrete values, is an imperishable possession of deity, "to whom all hearts are open and from whom no secrets are hid," including emotional secrets and hidden beauties of a person's inner life. (Strange that the quoted lines from the Anglican prayer book have meant so little to theologians as they evidently did for some centuries.)

We come at last to the sixth topic, revelation. Is it not clear that the two opposites here are, on the one hand, that there is an absolutely infallible, yet humanly accessible, special source of knowledge in religion, and on the other, that there is no source of such knowledge deserving of any trust or confidence whatever? We should remember that scientists do not claim any result of science as absolutely certain as it stands, yet our engineers apply many such results with confidence. Similarly, granted that there are no absolutely infallible sources of religious knowledge, this does not imply that any Tom, Dick, Susan, or Mary is as likely to be of help as the saints or religious founders of history, or that any book you please is as likely to be wise religiously as the Bible, the Buddhist Sutras, or the Bhagavad Gita. Between no revelation and absolutely certain and reliable revelation there can be many gradations.

Of all claims to infallibility, those made by fundamentalist Christians seem the most extreme. Certainly they are the most complex in their implications. With the religion of Islam, for instance, one only has to believe in the divine inspiration of one man as absolutely reliable. But with Christianity there are, for instance, the four authors of the Gospels, none of whom, as I recall, explicitly claims infallibility, several writers of *Epistles*, the author of the Acts of the Apostles, and many authors of the Old Testament. All must be supposed infallible, though again they do not clearly claim this status for themselves, so far as I can see.

What does it mean to regard authors as incapable of error? The writers must, it seems, be supposed absolutely controlled (when writing) by divine power. This notion of absolute control is the notion of omnipotence criticized under topic 2. I suggest that it is a nonidea. That we can learn about God from a book is one proposition, that we can learn to be infallible about God from a book, or from anything else, is a very different proposition. From an infallible God to an infallible book (to an infallible reader of the book?) is a gigantic step. For many of us it is a step from rational faith to idolatry. No book in a human language written by human hands, translated by human brains into another language, can literally be divine, "the word of God." What we know is that it is the word of human beings about God. The beings may be divinely inspired but they are still human.

In one of the Pauline letters the writer says that not all of his opinions come from Christ. This implies that some of the opinions may be mistaken. In general, claims of infallibility made for the Bible seem stronger than any made in the Bible.

The medieval Christian theologians were in their way scholars. Their view of biblical truth was less naive than the view of some fundamentalists. Not the Scriptures, as interpreted by someone who has merely been taught to read, are definitive of truth but the Scriptures as interpreted by the popes under carefully prescribed conditions. So it comes down finally at a given time to one human being in a special role in one human institution. Having read a *Catholic Encyclopedia* article on Infallibility, I still find the case for the view a weak one. The argument is that since human beings need a definitive guide in religion; a wise and benevolent God would give them what they need. The counter-argument is that humanity is the species of freely thinking animals who cannot simply set aside their thinking powers, frail and mistake-prone as these are, and directly and infallibly incarnate divine wisdom. What such animals need is to learn methods, as in the sciences or philosophy, of cooperation and mutual correction by which they can at least approach the truth, and methods of give and take, mutual respect, compromise, and kindness, by which they can compose their conflicting purposes without unnecessary frustrations and injury to one another.

A notable feature of the classical or medieval view was the belief that in Greek philosophy there had been an approximation, by human reason without special revelation, to the truths of revealed religion. So when the Church Fathers read the Scriptures they expected to find what they took to be the essential principles of the Greek way of thinking, with some additional truths peculiar to the Judaeo-Christian tradition. Biblical texts, admittedly with some qualifications, were expected to have a meaning that made sense in terms of the only philosophy these men knew. Among the especially relevant texts were those that referred to God as perfect or as unchangeable.

In the English Bible there are many occurrences of the words 'perfect,' 'perfectly,' or 'perfection.' Most of these are used to describe, not God, but certain human individuals, either as they are or as they ought to be. They are perfect, not in every conceivable respect, but in ethical or religious goodness, faithfulness in living by the religious code. Perfection in physical beauty, skill, or worldly knowledge is simply not in question. Thus the all-round metaphysical meaning of absolute value is not intended. How is it with the rare uses of 'perfect' or 'unchanging' to describe God? In every case the context implies something other than the Greek metaphysical idea of "in no respect capable of change or increase." Thus, the Malachi passage (3:6), "I Jehovah change not," where 'perfect' does not occur, clearly asserts the absolutely reliable, unwavering goodwill of Jehovah toward the people of Israel. (Turn again to me and I shall . . ."). Similarly, "Ye shall be perfect as your heavenly Father is perfect" (Matt. 5:48) is far from the use of words to indicate an absolute difference between divine and human forms of being, the one simply perfect, the other simply imperfect.

God, to be sure, is in goodwill entirely, always, and without possibility of failure beyond criticism, while we are so only inconstantly and more or less. The essential point concerns, not change as such, in ethically neutral or positive, as well as negative, respects, but only change from good to bad (or mediocre) and back again. The metaphysical question is not raised. Biblical authors were not metaphysicians. But the Church scholars, for instance Augustine, steeped in Greek philosophy, looked for metaphysics everywhere—and thought they had found it. Yet in fact the concept of supreme or divine reality as "unmoved mover" (Aristotle) was not a topic in New or Old Testaments.

"Without shadow of turning" (James 1:17) is preceded and followed by discussions of ehtical matters and of God as the One from whom all good things come. The beneficence of deity is thus the topic. Again this is not metaphysics, or a general definition of God. Spinoza was right, the Bible is no treatise in philosophical theology. The Malachi passage even suggests that, without prejudice to the divine goodness, there is divine change, for if Israel returns to fulfilling the divine commandments God will correspondingly, that is, will change in ways entirely appropriate to the change in Israel. Many parts of the Bible, interpreted reasonably, imply this.

For the Church Fathers divine knowledge eternally, timelessly surveys all events in time, whether past or future to us. Much in the Old Testament seems to imply a quite different view, and no Biblical passage, I believe, definitely and unambiguously implies a completely unchanging divine survey of all time. The Biblical scholar Oscar Cuhlman has dealt with this matter. The new theism can come closer to biblical ideas than was possible in the Dark or Middle Ages.

Classical theology was a compromise between a not-very-well-understood Greek philosophy and a not-very-scholarly interpretation of sacred writings. Omnipotence as many construed it is not asserted (indeed it is denied) by Plato and Aristotle, nor is it unambiguously affirmed in Scriptures. As for immortality (as the denial that a human career terminates at death) Plato held the doctrine but Aristotle did not. Moreover, Plato's (or Socrates') argument for his view on this point is not considered impressive by very many philosophers today. In most of the Old Testament the view is not affirmed but by implication denied.

The classical view of revelation is not convincing to very many scientists, philosophers, or humanists of our time. As we learn more about the claims of the non-Christian, non-Judaeic religions, it becomes ever harder to see how the extreme doctrine of infallible sacred writings can be sound. To insist upon that doctrine imposes a fearful burden on our democracy. It was not an accident that the founders of our republic were far from fundamentalist Christians. Jefferson, Franklin, Ethan Allen, Lincoln, and still others were believers in God but not in the infallibility of any book or human institution. The same is true of Emerson, our great poet whose prose was more poetic than most verse. It holds also for Peirce, James, and Royce, three of our greatest philosophers. Is it desirable that religion should seem more and more an affair of the intellectually undistinguished or mediocre?

The Principle of Dual Transcendence

The first four of the mistakes dealt with above are "one-sided" views in that they seek to distinguish God from all else by putting God on one side of a long list of contraries: finite-infinite, temporal-eternal, relative-absolute, contingent-necessary, physical-spiritual, and still others. But this is a species of idolatry, implying that what we worship is infinity, eternity, absoluteness, necessity, mere spirituality, or disembodied mind. But these are empty abstractions. So is love, if you only mean the mere quality of lovingness. What is really worshipful is the love which is infinite in whatever sense that is an excellence and is finite in whatever sense that, too, is an excellence. God contrasts with creatures, not as infinite with finite, but as *infinite-and-finite (both in uniquely excellent ways,* beyond all possible rivalry or relevant criticism) contrasts with the merely fragmentary and only surpassably excellent creatures. God contrasts with creatures, not as the merely absolute contrasts with the relative, but as the absolute-and-relative in uniquely excellent ways contrasts with the creatures as neither relative nor absolute, except in senses in which they are surpassable by others. God is similarly both eternal and temporal in all-surpassing ways; God alone has an *eternal individuality,* meaning unborn and undying, and God alone has enjoyed the entire past and will enjoy all the future. He-She is both physical and spiritual, and the divine body (see the next chapter) is all-surpassing and all-inclusive of the creaturely bodies, which are to God as cells to a supercellular organism. His-Her spirit embraces all the psychical there is with all-surpassing, unstinted love.

The idea of omnipotence, as usually construed, contradicts dual transcendence; for it means that God is wholly active, independent, or absolute in relation to the creatures and that the creatures are wholly passive in relation to God. It means that God does either everything or nothing. If everything, then the creatures do nothing and are nothing. The divine excellence is a uniquely excellent way of interacting with others, of being active *and* passive in relation to them. We do things to God by deciding our own being, with necessary help from God, as setting limits to the disorder inherent in freedom, and as inspiring us to take our place in the cosmic order as best we can. God loves us as we partly make ourselves to be, not simply as we are divinely made to be. To say that a lover is uninfluenced by a partly self-made loved one is nonsense or contradiction. Omnipotence was often taken in a way that amounts to that contradiction.

The formula "dual transcendence" is mine. The basic idea is in Whitehead and still others, but in some respects less sharply formulated. The criticism, made for instance by a conservative English theologian, that it is contradictory to attribute both finitude and infinity, for example, to the same deity is nothing but the neglect of an elementary logical truth, which is that the description of something as both P and not-P (where P is some predicate or property) is contradictory *only* if the predicate and its negation are applied in "the same respect" to the something in question. And dual transcendence does not make or permit such an application. Moreover, it offers a definite explanation of how the difference in the two respects is possible. The absolute, infinite side is abstract and concerns the divine potentiality or capacity to have values, while the finitude or relativity concerns the divine actuality. If you or I had made different decisions, God would have enjoyed (or suffered) these other decisions. Anything that could be actual God could divinely have, but what God actually has depends partly on creaturely decisions. This is the social structure of existence. The primacy of love means that there is no possible value that any being could have simply in and by itself, or simply by its own decision.

Aristotle said that the abstract or universal is real only in the concrete and individual. But he failed to realize how abstract and merely universal was his idea of God, defined as unmoved mover changelessly thinking—thinking what? The divine thinking, Aristotle said, was simply thinking thinking itself. Particular things or individuals, such as you or me, are not worth knowing about. Only eternal essences, universals, are worth knowing. And so if we know both the universal essence human, and this or that particular human person, we know what God does and something more besides. The Greek fascination with abstractions and disparagement of the concrete could not have been better displayed than in this paradox. Of course few theologians, least of all Christian theologians, could so disparage the worth of individuals when even a sparrow is said in the Gospels to be of interest to the Heavenly Father. But the theologians failed, on their part, to realize what Aristotle had seen very clearly, that if, contrary to Aristotle's opinion, God is aware of particular individuals and their careers, then the entire fullness of reality must be embraced in divine knowledge. But this concrete fullness is not eternal, it receives new items moment by moment. Also some at least of the items are contingent, results of free decisions, divine or creaturely, or both. Hence it will no longer do to hold that God is exclusively eternal and necessary, rather than also temporal and contingent. Like it or not, the door to the doctrine of dual transcendence has been opened.

We do not contradict ourselves if we say that a certain person is unchanging in being always (reasonably) "kind," although of course in concrete particulars responding differently to take changing circumstances into account. The idealized form of this contrast can be applied to God, who alone can unfailingly conform to the ideal of kindness.

That there are really different aspects of the divine nature, as dual transcendence implies, will be rejected by some thinkers on the ground that God is "simple," a traditional doctrine. But as used against dual transcendence, this argument would be purely question-begging. God is both simple and complex, the one in abstract, the other in concrete aspects. For instance, the divine cognitive infallibility is not really different (illustrating simplicity) from the divine ethical infallibility. But the aesthetic value actualized in God is no mere infallibility of the divine aesthetic capacity to respond. Aesthetic value, unlike merely cognitive or ethical value, depends in part upon what is responded to. It is concrete. There is a real difference (illustrating complexity) between the absolutely unsurpassable cognitive perfection of God's knowing, or the absolute rightness of the divine decision-making about the creatures, and the beauty of the actual, cosmic poem (the "verses" of which are partly self-decided) as divinely enjoyed.

Paul Tillich's "God is being but not *a* being," that is, universal but not individual, violates dual transcendence and is open to the objections to be made against all such violations, that they either make God an empty abstraction, or else make Him-Her a fetish, a *merely* finite, relative, and changeable individual . A merely finite God of course will not do. The only infinity some of us can see as making sense we do attribute to God, but not the meaningless, contradictory, or empty *mere* infinity of the traditional view.

Since the fifth and sixth mistakes are not about the uniquely exalted nature or function of God but about the special nature or status of our human species, dual transcendence does not apply to these latter topics—unless our species is indeed transcendent, an infinite exception in nature, supernatural in the sense in which God is. And that is precisely the issue between the traditional view and the new view of immortality. Like all animals we have finite careers between birth and death; but the old view of immortality holds that we have infinite careers after death. This is an extreme view. The opposite extreme is that after death our careers become less than finite, they become reduced to zero. As corpses we have no sequence of live experiences, finite or infinite. We are dead and unconscious. What was something is now nothing. Yet how can the same reality be both something and nothing? The modest but positive view of immortality is that our years of aliveness will always be just that.

Ask yourself, what is Julius Caesar now? That Caesar is "not now alive" means that while Caesar's experience and action are still having influence on our present world and ourselves, we and our world are having no influence on Caesar. Our contemporaries are those we can interact with; our ancestors still do things to us, but never can we do anything to them. This is the meaning of the nonexistence of past individuals. They are still real, but their causal relations to us as realities are one-sided, whereas our relations to one another are two-sided. Death and the passage of time destroy no concrete realities; for the concrete consists of events: not persons or things, but persons or things at given moments. Caesar at a certain moment in the first century B.C. will always be just that. The full value of this can be appreciated only by a believer in God, for whom the whole past is as vividly still enjoyed as a second ago is for us, or rather, more vividly than that.

The question of revelation also involves two extremes or one-sided views, with the truth intermediate. God, who is infallible, communicates with us, who are fallible. The message sender cannot err, but the message receiver can err. Result, the message *as received* is neither absolute possession of truths about God nor absolute nonpossession of such truths. It is fallible, suggestive, vague, but still genuine possession of more or less definite truth. It is a help to our weak, uncertain, partial awareness of what God is. To know God as certainly and distinctly as God knows God is a divine privilege, not a human one. Let us not pretend to be other than human.

Our distinction, compared to the other animals, is not that we have infinite careers while they have finite ones, or absolute knowledge of God while they cannot have any sense of God. It is that we alone enjoy the conscious understanding of our finitude, we alone definitely distinguish ourselves now from ourselves a year ago and yet see a partial identity between the two selves, we alone can definitely plan our careers, relate them (however inadequately) to the career of the human species and to God; we alone can be conscious in this life that after death our lives as lived will everlastingly remain still vividly real to God in whatever beauty they had. We alone can have definite thoughts about God and can reasonably believe that these thoughts are approximations to at least partial truths about God. Our superiority to the other animals is not absolute (only God is absolutely exalted above others), but ours is an *immense relative* superiority, as the mass of all human poetry ever written is immense compared to the no-poetry-at-all (unless in some extremely attenuated sense) of the other animals. Or consider the mass of human music (during who knows how many thousands, perhaps tens or hundreds of thousands, of years) compared to the much simpler music of birds and those few mammals who can be said to sing (gibbons, humpbacked whales, and a few others), not to mention the extremely limited singing of insects, frogs, toads, and a few lizards. Our superiority, viewed soberly, is sufficient, without our feeling it necessary to resort to fairy tales to enhance it. Consider the vast distance between any knowledge the chimpanzees could be said to have of the world around them and our sciences, surveying the cosmos over billions of light years and back to the Big Bang. How conceited do we have to be to try to claim more preeminence than that which we know of ourselves *in this life?*

The supernatural is real; but the supernatural is God, not humanity. In the supernatural reality of God, unbounded in space, unborn and undying, the bounded, fragmentary reality of each of us is imperishably included, a definite quantum in the Life which is all-in-all, or in which "we live and move and have our being" (*Acts of the Apostles:* 17, 28).

Chapter 2
The Physical and the Spiritual

Materialism and Dualism in Greek and Medieval Thought

THE WESTERN WORLD until modern times had two principal views about the place of mind in the world, by 'mind' meaning such processes as feeling, thinking, remembering, experiencing, and the like. According to the dominant view, there were two basically different aspects or kinds of reality, mind and matter, or souls and bodies. (From the Greek word *'psyche'* for soul comes the word 'psychology'; I shall sometimes use 'psychical,' in contrast to 'physical,' for mind in contrast to mere matter.) The general belief was that much of nature consists of mere matter, the merely physical, entirely lacking in mind—unless the divine mind, said to be everywhere, ubiquitous, somehow comes in. Thus rocks, water, or air. However, in the living parts of nature there is something additional called 'soul.' In plants this is what Aristotle called vegetable soul, lacking feeling or thought but having power to preside over the growth of the organism. With animals the soul is at least sentient, able to feel; with humans it is conscious, able to think and know. This scheme may be called 'dualism.' To be sure, the two aspects, soul and body, were not merely coordinate. Body was everywhere, soul was localized (apart from God). On the other hand, in the theistic systems, which most systems were, mind or soul in supreme form, God, was creator of, or at least supreme power over, everything. To that extent, psychology rather than physics was dominant, if we include in psychology the theory of the divine nature as supreme form of the psychical or spiritual. One did not talk of a "psychology of God," but this was implied,

51

if God knows, thinks, or has purposes, and if we can theorize about these as divine attributes. Actually Berdyaev in this century may possibly have been the first to use the expression quoted in the previous sentence.

The harsh duality of mere body, in portions of nature, and body-with-soul in other portions was somewhat softened by a rather vague use of 'form' as found in mind and in the nonliving things. Thus a physical shape is a form, and so is a particular quality of sensation. I shall not stop to consider this complication. It tends to distract attention from the basic contrast I wish to consider, that between the supposedly merely physical and the psychical. I also will not consider the Stoic cosmology. I hold with Peirce that it was the weakest of the Greek systems.

The other view known in the West in early times, sharply formulated in Greece, was 'materialism,' accordingg to which reality consisted fundamentally and universally of atoms, infinitely hard lumps of 'matter' invisibly small, with unchanging sizes and shapes, moving about in empty space. Even a mind was but a swarm of a special kind of atom. This, taken literally, was not dualism but a materialistic or physicalistic monism. The influence of mind on matter, or vice versa, was, for this view, merely the interactions of atoms of one kind with atoms of other kinds. This was a neater theory of nature than any dualism can be. However, to mention only one difficulty, it is far from clear how mere differences of size, shape, and ways of moving about could constitute the difference between thoughts or feelings and mere insentient lumps of stuff. Greek materialistic atomism had no theology properly so called, but only a theory of immortal gods, such as Apollo or Venus, made up of special kinds of atoms whose organization into individual super-animal bodies was mysteriously indestructible and so immortal. Greek materialism seems to have had little effect on medieval theology unless it influenced Tertullian's doctrine that every individual, even God, has a physical aspect, a body. This doctrine does not seem to have influenced subsequent classical theism.

Plato's World Soul: The Mind-Body Analogy for God

Plato, the first systematic philosophical theologian in the West, perhaps in the world, was also, in the view of many, one of the wisest and best of such theologians. He regarded the universe as a divine body, animated by a divine soul called the World Soul. Superficially interpreted, Plato had two Gods, the purely eternal God, called the Demiurge, creator of all noneternal things including the World Soul itself, which was quasi-eternal and embraced in itself all other created things. A deeper interpretation, accepted by some scholars, holds that the purely eternal God is only an abstraction, an aspect of the World Soul ("Plato's real God"— Levinson), which is the concrete deity, with the Demiurge that same Soul considered merely as having an eternal ideal which it is forever engaged in realizing by a process called "a moving image of eternity." Since self-creation or self-making is a basic idea in neoclassical theism, the idea that the Soul, utilizing the partly self-created creatures, creates its own forever unfinished actualization is a tempting way to read Plato. The Soul is aware not only of the eternal ideal but of the noncosmic animals, including us, and their lesser souls. Strict omniscience in the classical sense of surveying all events, no matter how future to us, is not, I think, an idea to which Plato is committed.

Alas, Plato's wisdom was only partly taken advantage of in later developments. If he perhaps influenced Tertullian in that writer's assertion of a divine body, later thinkers for two thousand years seem mostly not to have taken the hint. Nor did they appreciate Plato's discretion in viewing God's power as that of "persuading" the creatures, who do not completely enact into concrete actuality the divine ideal. Plato seems uncertain whether the incomplete control of things by God arises from "matter" or from the freedom ("self-motion") of created souls (the latter being the neoclassical view). In any case Plato was not burdened with the most egregious form of the problem of evil. The medieval theologians were less judicious. They made God a disembodied spirit with power to determine all becoming, or at least failed to make clear how they avoided this catastrophic conception.

It is fairly obvious that Plato's "two Gods" doctrine in some degree anticipated Whitehead's "primordial" and "consequent" natures of God and my principle of dual transcendence. The twentieth-century "process theology" is in some respects a return to Plato, after a very long detour.

To appreciate the idea of a divine body, we need to remind ourselves that any idea of God must in some way make use of analogies, or at least metaphors, in attempting to show how our idea of the radically superhuman can nevertheless be our human idea. We have no alternative to the use of comparisons with phenomena in our experience. These fall basically, for theological purposes, into two kinds or classes. There is the class of interpersonal relations. Thus God is thought of as related to a creature as a parent to its child or as a ruler to a subject or citizen of a country. Other variations are the teacher-pupil relation, or a writer and director of plays as related to the actors and actresses who perform the plays, or a musical composer-conductor as related to the musicians performing the music. In Judaea only the interpersonal analogy seems to have been actually used. In Greece Plato offered a very different one, the relation of a person as soul or conscious individual to the physical body of that individual. His suggestion was largely ignored, for instance by his disciple Aristotle, and by the scholastics generally. I think that in this they were sadly mistaken. I shall now explain why.

Interpersonal relations, whether those of parent to child or of ruler to ruled, have two serious limitations as bases for a divine-human analogy. As soon as a child is born, it begins a long process of *separation* from its mother, and it has always, even in the womb, been separated from its father. But the divine is that which is "nearer to us than breathing and closer than hand or foot." The intimate sustaining presence of deity is very feebly suggested by the parent-child relationship. The other limitation of interpersonal relations for theological purposes is that the radical *inferiority* of human beings in comparison with deity is only weakly or misleadingly modeled by that of a child in comparison with its parent. True, the child at birth, or as a mere infant, still more before birth (*pace* pro-lifers) is indeed far from equal, in intelligence or according to any standard measure of value, such as moral goodness, to a normal parent. But a healthy child talking with some fluency, showing kindness and sympathy with other children or its parents, is already beginning almost to rival adults in some virtues, values, or powers.

To furnish anything like an analogy to the vast contrast, and the impossibility of rivalry, between a human person and deity, one must follow the production of the child all the way down to the fertilized egg cell. A person or higher animal is at least a (very complex) multicellular creature, a metazoan. The egg cells is so only in potentiality. Actually it is no metazoan, and the facts that it was produced by metazoan animals and could be enabled, *with a vast deal of help*, to become such an animal, cannot with intellectual honesty be equated with simply *being* such an animal. As the Buddhists for two thousand years have seen, "A can turn into B" is one thing, "A is B" is another. (So long as pro-lifers persist in denying this distinction, than which none could be much plainer, my conclusion must be that they are trying to prove their case by verbal ambiguity.) Even a small child is enormously superior to a fertilized egg or any single cell whatever, for the child is many billions of such cells, a substantial portion of them organized into a nervous system, the most complex, subtly integrated natural system we know about, short of God as the integrated cosmos!

Inferior as the early pre-child stage of a human offspring is to its parent, it is still not by itself an adequate basis for trying to conceive our relation to deity. The fetus is radically separate from its male parent, and even in relation to its mother it is to a considerable extent on its own. In later stages it could conceivably be in an incubator and still grow into a child, physically regarded.

Now turn back to the mind-body analogy. Here indeed we have something like what we need. Each cell in our body is almost as nothing in comparison with ourselves as conscious individuals. Yet each may contribute something directly to our awareness, at least each cell in our brain's cortex may do so. The brain, or perhaps the central nervous system, is a sort of body within the body, the quintessential body. Between our experiences and our central nervous systems (or, if you will, our brains) there is no further mediating mechanism. *How* we feel, and *how* certain nerve cells act, depend somehow directly on each other. If we think or feel in wrong ways, bodily ills may quickly follow; if our cells internally function badly, we feel the harm as our own. What is pain, some of us wonder, if not our participation in cellular damage or discomfort? As David Hume rightly remarked, if anywhere in our world mind acts directly on body (and vice versa) it is in nervous systems. God must act directly on each creature, not merely via other creatures. The mind-body, or mind-nerve-cell, analogy is *all we have* for this, apart from rare and controversial cases of table rapping and the like. How can theology justify neglecting this unique form of creature-creator analogy?

Male Bias in Theology

Theologians thought that the mind-body analogy implied a degrading view of deity. They forgot (when so thinking) that the father analogy can similarly be regarded as degrading. Does God have a male sex organ? Yet without that organ what is left of the idea that, as God causes the world, so the father causes the child. The grim joke of the matter is that our forefathers were under the utterly wrong conviction that the physical origin or "seed" which is the beginning of the offspring is solely from the father. Their excuse, but not by any means justification, was their ignorance of the female egg cell, without which no child comes to be. Each child comes from *two* seeds, one from father and the other from mother. Male chauvinism has, as one origin, the sheer mistake of denying the female egg cell! The theory (one finds it in Aristotle) was that the mother furnishes merely the soil in which the seed is planted. The father furnishes the "form," the mother the mere "matter." The father is thus the real cause of the child, not the mother. I say that this is only excused, not justified, by ignorance. For there was not a scintilla of evidence that the mother's ovaries and egg cells and their functions did *not* exist. Sheer ignorance was turned into a theory insulting to women. My sex cannot justify this procedure. At best it can ask to be excused.

I have even understated the case against the traditional view of the father as sole origin of the offspring. All experience shows that in form children are as likely to resemble mothers as fathers. Aristotle's theory is *against* the evidence, not merely unsupported by it. Why was Aristotle so sure of his father-favoring theory?

Had the male half of the species made somewhat more use than it seems to have of its vaunted capacity for rational objectivity, a capacity it has sometimes accused women of lacking, it might have realized that at least a partial, and for all anyone can easily prove, fairly complete explanation of the fact that women have not been close rivals to men in most of the arts and sciences of civilization is not something women are born *without* and men *with* but the opposite, something men are born without and women with. This is the capacity and hence obligation to assume 99 percent of the not-light task of reproducing the species, plus the more arbitrary cultural imposition of tasks that the men and women are born equally capable of, such as preparing food and spinning, weaving, and sewing garments. When we find the sainted Thomas Aquinas saying, "What makes a woman a woman is her inability to produce semen," we see what the medieval score is in this matter of sexism.

A *few* men—Ralph Waldo Emerson, a hero of my youth, John Stuart Mill, and some male playwrights and novelists—stand out as exhibiting in the last century the disinterested rationality about the division of labor between the sexes that most men and all too many women have long lacked and, alas, some still have not yet acquired. How much more reasonable it would have been had Aquinas said that what makes a man a man is his physiological inability to bear and by his own bodily product nourish children!

In fairness it should be said that so long as the medical and hygienic knowledge and technical resources needed to lower the death rate, and therefore the desirable birth rate, were lacking, and women were forced to bear and care for, on the average, a large number of children and to spend most of their adult lives doing that, it was not in human weakness to see what a difference it would make to the lives of women when the death rate of the young was drastically lowered, and in addition women's longevity greatly extended. These and other quantitative changes resulting from applied science have qualitative implications. This is what the feminist movement of recent times is all about. Like other movements, it has its share of fanatics. But the changed basic conditions are realities and must be faced, well or ill. Women must still perform the primary part of the bearing of children; but they no longer need to see this task as their only important adult function. Indeed, it is not in the interest of men any longer that they should do so. The world does not suffer from a dearth of babies, and women cannot give men the companionship they need if being mothers is alone on their minds—that and being men's mistresses.

The mind-body analogy is not degrading if the father (or parental) analogy is not. And without either analogy there is no good basis for the idea of God as causative of creatures.

Creation from Nothing, Magic, and the Tyrant Conception of God

There is one phenomenon that has some resemblance to what seems to be meant by the classical (but not Greek) idea that God causes the world, not out of some already existent entity but "out of nothing." This is the phenomenon or supposed phenomenon of magic. God said, "Let there be light," and there was light. The magician says, "Abracadabra," and the genie comes out of the bottle. To be sure, the magician saying "Abracadabra" is not disembodied spirit; his speech is done by his body. However, one can think of a magician or of God producing the result by merely *thinking* something. What it comes to is that for the creation-out-of-nothing idea there was no *noncontroversial* analogous phenomenon whatsoever. It was a human concept, or supposed concept, with no basis in well-attested human experience. Yet what fateful consequences sprang from this so oddly and insecurely based idea! The matter is too important for exclusive reliance to be placed on such a semantic quicksand as the supposed occurrence of purely magical causation.

The feminists' complaint that they have been asked to worship a male deity seems pertinent and well founded. "Men are the masters" easily fits the tyrant conception of God, whose function is to command while the creatures merely obey. But how if the command is, as Berdyaev suggested, "Be creative and foster creativity in others." Then God as all-creative, all-determining Cause, effect of, influenced by, nothing, is no longer an appropriate idea. Much more appropriate is the idea of a mother, influencing, but sympathetic to and hence influenced by, her child and delighting in its growing creativity and freedom.

Lincoln said, "As I would not be a slave, so I would not be a master." Is Lincoln to be considered nobler than God? Would God be a master, in the sense some have given this term, a cosmic sovereign? Tyrannical people may worship a tyrant God, but why should the rest of us do so?

Mind or Soul as Creative of Its Body

We are now ready to go more deeply into the Platonic analogy of soul and body. What is this relationship? Here Plato was somewhat baffled. All the world was then baffled by the problem of matter, which is still a wondrous conundrum. But physics and biology have thrown some light on it which the ancient world was without. We know, for instance, that the mind-body relation is not a one-to-one relation but a one-to-many relation. The body is a *society* of billions of cells, each a highly organized society of molecules and particles or wavicles. At a given moment each of us, as a conscious individual, is a single reality; but our body is no such single reality. Each white blood corpuscle is a tiny animal, each nerve cell is a single individual. Similarly, God's cosmic body is a society of individuals, not a single individual. The world as an integrated individual is not a 'world' as this term is normally and properly used, but 'God.' God, the World Soul, is the *individual integrity* of 'the world,' which otherwise is just the myriad creatures. As each of us is the supercellular individual of the cellular society called a human body, so God is the super-creaturely individual of the inclusive creaturely society. Simply outside of this super-society and super-individual, there is nothing.

Unlike the human bodily society, the divine bodily society contains not merely multitudes of radically subpersonal entities, such as cells or molecules, but also multitudes of multicellular plants and animals, including persons and those nearly personal creatures the apes and whales, and who knows what other forms of life on the astronomically probable billions of planets? Yet God is superior to all these in a manner of which the person-to-cell analogy gives only a faint idea. It is still, in some respects, a far better idea than that given by the merely interpersonal analogy of parent or ruler.

The "divine right of kings" never was really divine. The ancient Jews knew that, bless them. A king is only another human person, more by accident than intrinsic worth put in a position of power. But you or I as conscious individual is not just another cell in our bodily society. We do indeed rule over those cells by a sort of divine right, since it is the laws of nature, which for a theist are divinely instituted, that give us power to control our bodies, that is, power over our cells. The power of any one cell over us is as nothing compared to the power each of us has over multitudes of cells. We are quasi-deities in our bodily system. No parent has a comparable power over a child. In the womb a mother has only a vague, limited influence on the development of the fetus, compared to her influence on her own brain cells.

It is obvious enough, nevertheless, that if we take Plato's analogy seriously, and also the parent-to-child analogy, then it is the mother, not the father, who furnishes by far the best symbol of deity. The fetus-mother relationship is decidedly more intimate than the fetus-father relationship. Here, too, the male bias got things upside down.

I add with some diffidence that one reason for my hesitation to accept any of the recent (or old) theories of the incarnation of God in Jesus of Nazareth (some of the best of these theories being formulated by careful readers of my writings) is that any such theory at least strongly suggests the idea of deity as highly spiritualized masculinity. It is a constant temptation to male chauvinism, and a temptation in historical fact not altogether resolutely resisted, to put it mildly.

We come to the question: Does human experiencing in any sense create its brain cells? Here neurophysiologists disagree somewhat; but there are experts who hold that experiences exercise a creative influence upon the development of brain cells. Our every thought and emotion does things to those cells, which at birth are far from fully developed. Hence it is that an infant cannot even begin to learn to speak or to think (in the way made possible by language) until some months have passed. The human individual to some extent *presides over the coming to be of its cells.* A great Platonic poet, Edmund Spenser, expressed this idea, long before modern physiology:

> For the body from the soul its form doth take
> For soul is form and doth the body make.

The analogy between God-world and Soul-body can be carried yet further. Cells are like tiny animals; integrated individuals. Perhaps they are sentient individuals. There has long been a book (by the psychologist Binet, published in 1888) on *The Psychology of Microorganisms*. Why not a psychology of cells? True, apart from the white blood cells, our cells are not mobile. But it does not follow that they are inactive. They are constantly reorganizing their parts, repairing damage, and—except the nerve cells—dividing and thus reproducing their kind. No evidence, so far as I can see, supports the idea that cells are totally without anything like feeling. The feelings would concern chiefly their internal relationships and the stimuli they receive from their neighbors (in the case of nerve cells, across synaptic connections). They would not, unless in some extremely primitive sense, think or remember, but only feel. But what could show that they do not do even that?

It is arguable that we have direct evidence that cells do feel. For what is pain, physical suffering? It is fact that we feel pain when cellular harm is done. In shaving one often feels a slight twinge of pain and yet can see no cut in the skin. But wait a second, or two or three, and blood appears. Occasionally not, but is it not reasonable to think then of imperceptibly slight skin damage? If it is fact that our suffering means cellular damage, what is the simplest explanation of our feeling of suffering? Surely the simplest explanation is that our suffering is our immediate sharing in, sympathy with, something like suffering in the cells, which can give us feeling because they themselves have a kind of feeling that, when vaguely intuited by us, in indistinct, blurred fashion (so that we cannot consciously make out the individual cells, one by one), becomes our human kind of physical pain. We know that our awareness of cells (still more of molecules or atoms) is blurred, since we cannot identify the microindividuals as such. The hypothesis that sensation is indistinct but direct *sympathetic participation in cellular feeling* is the simplest explanation of human (and other higher animal) sensation that has been offered. One finds it (in different words) in Bergson, Peirce, Whitehead, and a few others.

Theologically the view has great advantages. For it makes sense at last of the ancient idea of love as the principle of principles. An American psychiatrist (I believe it was Karl Menninger) has quoted from an English author of the nineteenth century, "To sing the praises of love 'is to set a candle in the sun.'" The sun, I suggest, is the glow of that bond of sympathy which, as Plato hinted, holds the world together and relates the divine and the human. Our praise of this bond can indeed not appreciably add to its luster. But still, in the relative darkness of some theological discussions of love, the candle of our analysis may significantly increase the visibility.

Psychicalism and the Universality of Love

One more step. Even supposing that cells feel, we have the molecules, atoms, and still simpler constituents of nature to consider. Either the explanation in terms of sympathy, feeling of feeling, the root idea of love, goes to the bottom of things or it does not. If it does, then we have a coherent system of concepts applying theologically, psychologically, biologically, and physically. Otherwise we have a dualism of two ultimately different ways in which mind is related to what it experiences or knows, or in which individuals are held together to constitute a universe. This is an intellectual alternative; on one side a really thoroughgoing conceptual integration, on the other, a lack of such integration. Physicists, confronted by a dilemma of this sort, tend to favor, at least provisionally, the integral view. They tend to dislike dualisms. I recall a physicist expressing disgust for the idea that nature consists first of the merely physical, devoid utterly of life, and then of the physical plus an absolutely new principle of life. More and more, physicists dare to say that all nature is in some sense life-like, that there is no absolutely new principle of life that comes in at some point in cosmic evolution.

If this drive for conceptual integration proves irresistible, as I suspect it may, then we shall see *either* a universal materialism (or physicalism) or a universal psychicalism. The negative concept of mindless, insentient stuff or process (apart from special and exceptional cases) will be accepted as the universal principle of reality; *or* mind in a most generalized sense will be accepted as that principle. I suggest that theology must favor the second solution. Then love will relate God not only to human beings but to all creatures, and will apply to the soul-to-bodily-cells relationship and, in its ultimate generality, to all relationships of creature to creature, creature to Creator, Creator to creature. Of the two escapes from dualism, materialism and psychicalism, the latter has clear advantages. It is the more intelligible monism.

To the six theological mistakes described in Chapter 1 we can now add a seventh: theology should not accept the idea of mere, insentient, lifeless, wholly unfree matter. Materialism and an absolute mind-matter dualism are implicitly atheistic doctrines.

Chapter 3
Creation through Evolution

Evolution and Belief in God

ABOUT 1914, WHEN I was seventeen years old, Dr. Gardner, an Episcopal clergyman and my science teacher at Yeates boarding school (now only a memory in a few minds), introduced me to the theory of evolution. I remember no details; but since Gardner was in every way, as I had sufficient opportunity to know, a religious man, he must have interpreted evolution positively and as compatible with his theological beliefs. Had he attacked it on that ground I would certainly have been keenly interested and concerned and would have remembered the conflict thus brought to my attention. The fact is that I do not recall knowing anything in my teens about the supposed incompatibility between evolutionary biology (what other biology is there?) and belief in God. I may or may not have known then that my father, probably before I was born, had accepted the basic idea of evolution. He, too, was an Episcopal minister; like Dr. Gardner, he was not a fundamentalist, that is, not a Christian who confuses worship of God with worship of a certain set of ancient documents written (and translated) by human beings. A year or two later, at Haverford College, a Quaker institution, a young instructor taught, in a class in which I took part, a fairly sophisticated version of neo-Darwinism. Again I saw nothing irreligious in the theory. I still see nothing irreligious in it, though I now have some understanding of the several reasons why many think otherwise.

In the Southwestern American city in which I now live, one can frequently read in the local newspaper letters insisting that there are only two options: evolution without God, or God without evolution. In fact, of course, millions of believing Christians, and a still larger number of believers in God, also accept the basic tenets (not, of course, every detail of some current scientific formulation) of evolutionary biology. I suspect that most European Christians do so. In my long academic life I have known hundreds of scientists (especially ornithologists), numerous theologians, and numerous philosophers; yet an anti-evolutionary scientist, theologian, or philosopher has not come my way. I've heard one or two on radio or television, and I once met a fanatical Canadian college student who claimed to know just how false evolution was; but, on the whole, anti-evolutionary scientists, philosophers, and theologians are for me almost fictitious entities. I did come to know an Australian school teacher of biology, an excellent observer of birds in the field, who argued against evolution—but not on what seemed very cogent grounds.

The history of nonevolutionary biology is not merely the story of fundamentalist Christian opponents of evolution. Aristotle was a prime example. Immanuel Kant was another; his (pre-Darwinian) opposition was emphatic. And I regard this aspect of Aristotle's and of Kant's thought as a weakness, and in Aristotle's case even an inconsistency, in their world-views. In recent philosophy, anti-evolutionism is hard indeed to find. It is in regions or circles where philosophy counts for little, as in some parts of this country, that evolution is supposed vulnerable to easy attack. In scientific and philosophically literate circles the argument seems about over. Must religion be a last retreat from knowledge?

There are any number of open questions as to specifics about evolution, but they are neutral to the issue between evolution as such and fundamentalist "creation science." Moreover, the "creation scientists" (supposing for the argument that the phrase makes sense) disagree, too, on specifics. Some say that there may be evolution of species but not of genera (or is it of genera but not of families, or families but not of orders, or orders but not of classes—birds, say, or mammals?). After all, the brief account or accounts (are there not two?) in Genesis are vague as to definite species (other than the human), or even as to genera or families. To call 'science' a view whose only definite evidences are what can be read into a certain book has no reasonable connection with what practicing scientists mean by the word. This has, in a way, been admitted by some spokespersons for creation "science." They say that their view is a philosophy. But this usage too has little connection with what practicing philosophers understand by that word. I say it is bad philosophy, bad science, bad theology, and bad hermeneutics (textual interpretation), and no good thing at all.

Evolution, Chance, and Natural Law

First, the philosophical question. A philosopher may believe in God and many have done so and do. But philosophers do not now make statements about "the word of God," as though God uttered or wrote sounds or words of some human language for us to hear or read. There is, however, a genuine philosophical question about the religious meaning of evolution. According to the tyrant idea of God, there is no element of *chance* in reality. Everything is deliberately and precisely arranged by divine wisdom and power. According to the evolutionary theory, offspring vary from their parents and from one another partly by chance. If evolution proceeds in a fairly definite direction, it is because natural selection weeds out many nonadaptive chance variations, so that from very simple beginnings is woven a very complex "web of life," in which live many widely differing, but in their basic requirements mutually compatible, species. This web of life Darwin calls beautiful, and any good theory of beauty will justify this application of the word. I have argued this question elsewhere.

Presupposed in the foregoing is a basic set of physical laws setting limits to the reign of chance in nature, laws governing the behavior of the basic elements, especially hydrogen atoms. These laws are not explained by evolution. To suppose that Darwinism reduces the biological order to pure chance is thus a mistake. A basic physical order is assumed but not explained. Those of us who believe in God can suppose that this basic order is divinely decided. The numerous creatures could not get together and decide it. For the game of life there must be rules not established by any player, unless God is taken to be the supreme player.

It is known that the chance variations are not only the results of combinations of genes (units of inheritance) from the male and female parents. There are also "mutations," larger (mostly harmful) variations altering the genes themselves, and resulting from chance encounters between particles (such as cosmic rays) and the genes. As environments change, what was harmful may become useful and be retained through generations.

Presupposed by the theory is that the basic physical laws make it possible for cells (consisting of complex molecules highly organized into enduring systems) to exist and to reproduce themselves in a manner largely controlled by the structures called genes. Darwin did not know about these "bits of information" as to how new cells are to be made up. This lack greatly weakened his theory. Neo-Darwinism is a much stronger system. Never have subsequent discoveries done more to confirm the basic rightness of a concept than those since Darwin have to confirm his idea of natural selection. Mendel's laws of gene combination are exactly what Darwin needed in order to make the theory work without the assumption of the inheritance of acquired characters, for which (except in a sense to be discussed) empirical evidence was and is lacking.

Darwin's Mistake

Darwin used the very word 'chance' for his variations among offspring, but explained that he did not take this to be the whole truth of the matter. However, he also made it clear that the power of his theory to explain the evolution of species did not depend on belief in the absence of real chance and the presence of determining causes in nature. The biological explanation was, Darwin saw, a statistical matter. Given a huge number of generations, a fairly stable environment in inanimate nature, small variations due to combination of the dual inheritance from parents (plus mutations now and then), natural selection could in the long run and on the whole produce what we find. Whether by chance or not, the variations and mutations could, and according to the evidence did, do the required job.

What we have then is this. Darwin was a believer in causal determinism; but, as we know now, his theory works even better on a nondeterministic basis, such as those provided by quantum theory and the increasingly widespread general acceptance of statistical thought in science. Even before quantum theory the actually used laws of gases were already statistical, so that determinism did no real work even in that matter. The same was true of the entropy law in thermodynamics, and Willard Gibbs's phase rule in chemistry. Darwin in England, Gibbs in the United States, and others in Germany were participating—Darwin partly unknowingly—in a transformation of science away from determinism and toward a philosophy of chance limited by law. Neither pure chance nor the pure absence of chance can explain the world.

Chance, Freedom, and the Tyrant Idea of God

What is the theological significance of the foregoing? We have seen that chance is an inseparable aspect of freedom. Only those happy with the tyrant conception of deity can suppose that divine providence (creation or rule of the world) excludes chance. It merely limits the latter's scope. For example, a hydrogen atom may have certain degrees of freedom, but there are many things it cannot do. Again, for each type of unstable particle there are half-life laws. These never tell us precisely what an individual particle will do, but they tell us how long it will take (the length of time being specific to the type of particle) for half of a large group of particles of a certain type to change into some other type, or to disappear into energy. This mysterious-seeming *order in disorder* is, so far as we now know, the nature of the elementary constituents of the physical world.

If our previous analysis of the necessity for universal freedom of individual creatures is sound; if God is genuinely conceivable only as supreme freedom issuing in, dealing with, lesser forms of freedom; if the notion of creature as absolutely controlled, absolutely ordered puppet, is without positive meaning, except as the limiting or zero concept of an imagined series of less and less free individual creatures (what a creature would amount to if it amounted to nothing—if all this is true, then the present state of physics and biology is insofar theologically satisfactory. Everywhere, being a single creature can then mean making decisions among open possibilities, further determining the partially indeterminate tendencies constituting the future until it becomes present and then past.

Since genes too (or their dynamic constituents) are creatures, as are particles, they must be acting freely within limits, which means that the results are partly random, not predetermined by any intention or power. The only conception of providence which would exclude all chance would also exclude all decision-making creatures, which means, all creatures. Thus it would be "providence" without any world to provide for.

What kind of teleology (things arranged for the best) did Darwinism displace and discredit? It was that of a world order in which every monstrosity, every suffering, every birth of an unviable, ill-adapted animal was divinely decreed. The "problem of evil" in its most unmanageable form was the price of the view the bishops defended against Darwin. Moreover, Darwin saw this more clearly than the bishops did; he made it clear that he did not doubt the divine existence merely because of his evolutionary theory. His letters show this plainly. He said that the theologians had not, to his satisfaction, shown how the all-arranging power of God was compatible with the freedom of the creatures, particularly of human beings. He was right; they had not made a reasonable case on this point. But the difficulty was not primarily biological, it was theological. On purely theological grounds Darwin thought more cogently than the bishops mostly did. He said what they, on their own grounds, should have said. Or rather, he half said what they did not even half say.

What kept Darwin from successfully solving his own personal religious problem as to what to think about God was *not* his empirical biological discoveries. It was his a priori faith in the deterministic philosophy of science, which had reigned nearly unquestioned (even by theologians) in the Newtonian period, then nearing its end. What was theologically requisite was soon to prove scientifically acceptable. This was the admission that chance is a real aspect of nature in general. The theological relevance of this is simply that the denial of chance implies the denial of freedom, and the denial of freedom ruins theology.

God Takes Chances with Free Creatures

"God," said Einstein—who, like Darwin, could not admit the reality of chance—"does not throw dice." "On the contrary," said Arthur Young, an inventor important in the development of the helicopter,"God does play dice. To have creatures is to take a chance on what they may do." (This was in a conversation we once had.) This, I say, is good theology.

I ask the reader to recall that the evolutionary scheme presupposes an aspect of order in the world which it does not explain. To adapt to mere disorder is meaningless; and so the basic orderliness of the world cannot be explained by mutual adaptation among the creatures. That there are laws of nature is providential. Any cosmic order is infinitely better than none, for mere chaos is indistinguishable from nothing at all. But the only positive explanation of order is the existence of an orderer. Hence evolution is not, I hold, fully intelligible without God. And since God means supreme freedom dealing with lesser freedom, there must be a pervasive element of chance in nature. So the specifics of nature cannot be mere actualizations of a divine plan. The renunciation of strict determinism, which does no real work in science anyway, opens the door to a new form of theologizing, purified of the taint of divine tyranny which disfigured classical theology.

See James Joyce's *Portrait of the Artist as a Young Man* for a vivid picture of the dark side of classical theism. It has been shown that the sermon given in that book is no mere invention of Joyce's, but, almost word for word, an actual sermon written by a priest or monk of the Catholic church. There was a dark side of traditional religion, and Joyce very reasonably disliked it. The idea of God as supreme love enjoying (or, if you prefer suffering, or neutrally cognizing) the spectacle of sinners everlastingly punished for eternally predestined actions is not a pretty one; but there it is in classical theology. Darwin did better than he knew in helping to discredit it.

The Religious Opposition to Evolution

To form a judgment concerning the force of the evolutionary argument, one needs to have in mind a great mass of observational facts drawn from many branches of science: the study of fossils, the anatomy of plants and animals, the distribution of species over the earth's surface, evidences of changes in the earth's geology and climate, continental drift, the behavior of animals, and still others. One needs also to have considerable mathematical competence, since the issues are complex statistical questions of probabilities. Sewall Wright, a great evolutionist of this century, a person I know well as a careful, honest thinker, with no particular wish to undermine belief in God but a great wish to think and observe accurately throughout a long lifetime, possesses the requisite abilities and competences. He, like everyone else I know much about who, with anything like the same equipment and care, has gone into the matter, has no doubt that evolution has occurred. It is a great satisfaction to me that he is also a convinced psychicalist. If he is agnostic about God this is *not for biological reasons,* but because he finds it impossible to reconcile belief in God with his understanding of relativity physics. I appreciate his difficulty, which has bothered me for many years, as it has some other philosophers. I believe the difficulty is not decisive (and I am not alone in this), and in any case it is irrelevant to the biological issues.

Confronted with the attempt of believers in the literal infallibility of the Bible to dismiss the evidences of evolution, some of us feel a disgust such as Emerson expressed long ago in the following outburst:

It is not in the power of God to make a communication of his will to a Calvinist [the kind of fundamentalist that Emerson knew]. For to every inward revelation he holds up his silly book, and quotes chapter and verse against the Book-maker and Man-Maker, against that which quotes not, but is and cometh. There is a light older than intellect, by which the intellect lives and works, always new, and which degrades every past and particular shining of itself. This light, Calvinism denies, in its idolatry of a certain past shining.[1]

Today most of us would put more stress on observation and on logic than on Emerson's inward revelation, but we would agree with the charge of idolatry. God utterly transcends any book. As one of our founding fathers thought, it is nature, God's handiwork, that is the real "word of God" concerning the general structure of the cosmos. My clergyman father believed exactly that. I once heard another Episcopal clergyman (in Savannah, Georgia) say that to him science was revelation as truly as the Bible.

Not only is it difficult to believe that God literally took a rib from Adam and made it turn into Eve, but, as Clare Boothe Luce has well said, the human male was thus given the honor of being the mother of mankind, stealing from woman what in all honesty belongs to her.

God "Makes Things Make Themselves"

In what sense, granted evolution, can God be called Creator? Charles Kingsley, an English clergyman, beautifully puts it thus, in formulating the divine procedure: "I make things make themselves." Only so does a good parent, a good God, proceed. For the parent, or God, to do simply all the making is to leave no genuine function for the children to perform. Language supports this. We say that *we* "make" decisions, resolutions, or attempts, implying that God is not the unilateral maker or decider of literally everything. So the Socinians thought without quite saying it; so Lequier and Fechner thought, and they virtually did say it. Finally, Whitehead said it. And I believed it before his saying it, as my 1923 dissertation shows.

It is no mere accident that the linguistic analysts, influenced by Wittgenstein, have not noted the testimony of common speech in this matter. For their consideration of the "ordinary language" test has been applied selectively, under prejudices not altogether impossible to discern. We, finally, and not God, *make* decisions (mostly unconsciously) as to details of the lives of ourselves and our fellows. And so (according to the neoclassical view) do all creatures, though in still less conscious fashion in most of the natural kinds.

Does our making presuppose antecedently existing matter, while God's does not but is "from nothing"? I ask, in reply, "In making me did God use my parents or was I made simply from nothing?" I believe we can safely await an answer to this; for any answer will show the difficulty that classical theism faced. If my parents were not causally required for my existence, then we know nothing of the meaning of "cause." And if they were, then clearly I was not made from nothing. Our only knowledge of causation and of making is from the way what happens influences what happens next. True, we have an intuition of ourselves thinking—that is, 'making'—our thoughts or feeling our feelings, where the selves in question are simultaneous with the thinking or feeling. But if, analogically speaking, God's causing or making of the world is similar, then the world just is God's thinking, and surely that is not the intended meaning.

Recall once more the analogy with magic. God said, "Let there be light" and there was light. "Let there be . . .," and it was so. "Let there be . . .," and it was so. I have no quarrel with these verses from Genesis, but I deny that literalists understand their function. At the climax of the Book of Job (an inquiry into the ways of providence) we are told that a human being cannot understand God's creative power. Since we cannot understand it, neither science nor philosophy can make use of the idea to justify definite conclusions.

The origin of creation science is neither science nor philosophy. Nor is it intellectually responsible theology. Rather, it is poetry, and its function is to communicate feeling and express an attitude. God beheld what he had created and "saw that it was good." Somehow in response to divine decisions a good world order was coming into being. That it was coming into being preceded only by God, or by God and nothing, is not definitely asserted and, in view of the rebuke to Job, is not in order. We do not, in biblical terms, know how, or just with what, or without what, the creating is done. This is all beside the religious point, which is the reality of God as *somehow* voluntarily producing the basic world order and the essential *goodness* of the result. Also significant is the way God observes that result and *only then* "sees that it is good." According to classical theism, God first, or eternally, knows exactly what is to result and how good it will be; and the actuality is merely the planned good over again with no additional determinations. I regard this as a bad interpretation of the biblical account.

Creation Neither Out of Nothing Nor Out of Matter

What divine creation of a particular world order presupposes is neither a preexistent matter nor nothing at all. It is not matter; for that is a label for what, in the psychicalist view, is really an extremely elementary form of creaturely mind in the form of feeling, in huge numbers of momentary flashes with no conscious knowledge of individual identity through change. It is feeling uncomplicated by what Shakespeare once called "the pale cast of thought." In this sense it is unconscious, but *not* insentient. Creation's presupposition is not nothing; for there are difficulties with the idea of an absolute beginning of the creative process. There is no religious need for such a beginning, which limits God's productivity to a merely finite stretch of past results. This is not the only way in which the tradition, while talking much of the divine infinity, unduly *finitized* deity. The Buddhists wrote about a past of billions of billions of years, or an even huger number, while Europe talked about a mere several thousand years of past creating by deity. How childish this must seem to Buddhists, as it does to scientists!

Classical theism attempted to harmonize Greek philosophical and Judaic religious views. It is still desirable to search for harmony between the two traditions, but we need to use our additional resources in science, philosophy, and historical scholarship, including our vastly increased knowledge of the history of religions.

Taking Genesis and the Book of Job together, we may say that the biblical view was that the divine creativity is a highly mysterious matter. One may think of it by analogy with primitive magic, a notoriously superstitious affair. One may simply say that no humanly accessible analogy helps, that we just cannot have any rational theory at all here. This seems to be the message of Job. But that book had as author and (for all we know) intended readers only people whose culture was radically different from ours. It was prescientific and prephilosophical—as we, since the Greeks, have known philosophizing. So perhaps the veto on trying to theorize theologically need not without qualification apply to us. In fact, as some scientist has pointed out, part of the evidence by which the voice from the whirlwind convicts Job of inability to comprehend God's creating or ruling the world no longer applies. Science has thrown considerable light, for instance, on how animals manage to feed themselves or nourish their young. And we *can* lift leviathan out of the sea, even if not exactly with a fish hook. Above all, it is a thousand years too late to imply that, although God made human beings in the divine image, endowed with the ability to have definite (even though more or less abstract) thoughts about "all time and all existence" (as there is no ground for supposing even apes or porpoises can do), yet we are not to use our thinking capacity freely in seeking to learn about nature but must give absolute priority to the literal words of a book expressing thoughts that, it is only sensible to believe, were the thoughts of some remote human predecessors. And we are to have laws passed to impose this way (or at best to penalize a contrary way) of proceeding upon many who utterly reject the theory on which it is based. (The matter is—as Milton Friedman points out—gravely complicated by our primary reliance upon compulsion and governmental control in education. In so many ways we have feared to accept freedom as a guiding principle of life.)

Medieval thinkers went far beyond (or perhaps fell behind) biblical conceptions, using their understanding of Greek ideas. They thought they knew better than the naive writers of scripture what concepts do and what do not literally apply to deity. They were not fundamentalists in the current sense. However, if there is any consensus at all in scientific or philosophical—or even theological—circles in the matter, it is that the "medieval synthesis" was no permanent solution of the ultimate problems. It was pseudo-biblical and pseudo-Greek. If we make our own fresh try at the job, we may well partly fail too. But we need not be, as the Schoolmen were, Platonic yet largely lacking in much of the best of Plato's insight; Aristotelian yet lacking some of that thinker's most carefully worked-out ideas; Christian yet contradicting any natural interpretation of the heavenly parent of the Gospels and the Old Testament idea of the merciful Holy One.

In the Bible, God is just not an unmoved "pure actuality," in purely eternal fashion planning the very details of worldly existence. According to Genesis, the initial creative action took time—six "days," was it? At each stage God received new impressions of the goodness of the result. And then, as human beings came on the scene, God soon saw something not entirely good in the result and acted accordingly. Thus the God-world relations were not pictured as merely instantaneous but as a progressive and in some sense time-like succession. And there was *action and reaction* between Creator and creatures. There was the Covenant between God and Israel. The whole thing was a *social* transaction. Even the relations of God to "inanimate nature" seemed to take this form. The sea obeyed the injunction "thus far and no farther." The sun, "rejoicing as a giant to run his course," was no mere lump of dead matter. Since we now have a philosophy in which the social structure, fully generalized, is *the* structure of reality, we have less need than the Church Fathers had to explain away the social cast of biblical language. And we also have a philosophy (and science) in which creative becoming is taken as at least much more pervasive and more nearly ultimate than was possible with the overestimation of fixity and mere being which characterized Greek and medieval thought. So in that way too we can come closer than the Scholastics to agreeing with those naive scriptural writers above spoken of. Doubtless they were in some ways naive; but also, doubtless the Schoolmen had their own somewhat different form of ignorance or prejudice. We might do better than either group of predecessors, we who also are images of deity.

Classical theology paid insufficient attention, in reading Plato, not only to the mind-body analogy for God and the world, but also to the doctrine that the soul (any soul) is self-moved and that soul in its various forms is the explanation of all motion or change. Human or animal souls move themselves and their bodies, God moves God and all actualities, without fully determining any. Aristotle rejected the soul's self-motion and attributed change to matter in combination with mind. So his God, who (or which, for it is not a person) is wholly nonmaterial, is changeless and entirely uninfluenced by, as well as—and this was a consistent consequence—unaware of, the changes and accidental details of the world.

Aristotle was perhaps the first to state the intuitively satisfying principles: what comes to be is contingent (becoming produces genuine novelty and is in principle not wholly predetermined or preprogrammed); but what is without ever becoming is noncontingent, could not possibly not have been. It follows that in sheer eternity there is no freedom, but in becoming there is some freedom. But, while making this splendid contribution, Aristotle, by dropping Plato's insights about the World Soul, the cosmos as divine body, and the partially temporal nature of the World Soul, was unable to anticipate, as Plato did anticipate, the Judaeo-Christian-Islamic view of God as aware of the individual creatures. Aquinas and the other Schoolmen combined Aristotle's neglect of a not-wholly-immutable World Soul with the Platonic contention of God's knowledge of the creatures, thus losing Plato's consistency in asserting, and Aristotle's partial consistency in denying, God's knowledge of concrete, contingent reality. It was mediocre Platonism and mediocre Aristotelianism. And it was a biblical heresy.

It is true that the mind-body analogy does not immediately and in any very simple way show God can be the highest (though not the sole) creative power, the highest (though not the sole) decision maker. For although, by the Sperry psycho-physiological principle, the infant soul (or the infant experiencing) does begin to influence the becoming of the nerve cells—and less directly that of the other bodily cells—the early stages of the embryonic development must proceed without any infant psyche; for prior to the development of a nervous system there is no reason to attribute any such thing to the embryo. All that the facts indicate is cells multiplying and differentiating. The differentiations are in principle explained by the fact that different positions in the embryo expose cells to differing stimuli. The German biologist Driesch argued for a holistic entity directing cellular development, which he called an entelechy, but this has not proved a fruitful idea scientifically. And, in ordinary plants, which never do develop a nervous system, it is the cells that, to a botanist, explain growth, not something corresponding to the plant as a whole. A tree is a cell colony, not a single individual with integration comparable to that of each of its cells; as Whitehead put it, "a tree is a democracy." Its cells may have souls as little monarchs of their molecules, but probably not the tree a soul as monarch of its cells. So much for Aristotle's vegetable soul. It is not enough to say that he did not know about cells. Knowing nothing of the fact of cells, he implicitly denied them, just as in his male-favoring genetic theory he denied eggs to female human beings. I think a philosopher should know when he does not know, and avoid, better than this powerful mind did, implicit denials of things of whose existence or nonexistence he knows nothing.

As Soul of the cosmic body, God does not, like the infant, come to be out of a previous world state not involving Him-Her. Any stage of the cosmic body grew out of a previous stage already divinely besouled. This is the uttermost application of the analogy, the all-inclusive one. If the infant is slightly creative of its bodily cells after a certain stage in its body's development, God has already been and must always be, not slightly but supremely creative of the cells in the divine body, including you and me as such cells. Whitehead calls his view a "cell theory of reality" but never took the Platonic step of conceiving the cosmos as supreme body. I hold that in this he fell a little below Plato. The divine analogy to the human fails unless the mind-body relation applies on both sides to God. The human soul as disembodied is hopelessly unclear or false. A merely disembodied God is an unfounded idea. There is this much truth in naturalistic materialism. What we should be simply without bodies is gibberish. The great letter writer Paul knew that, so he posited a "heavenly body."

It may appear that the phrase "supremely creative," not only of recent stages of the worldly process but of all its predecessors, is not enough to make God the "creator of all things, visible and invisible." My proposition is simply that it is enough, *provided* you admit that the singular, concrete entities created are to have freedom, to be to some extent self-decided—"self-moved," as Plato put it. For then, as Kingsley said, what God does is to make things partly make themselves. Adam sinned: this was his decision, not God's. Indeed, the serpent's tempting of Adam was the serpent's decision, not God's. Job's torturers' acts, and even Satan's instigating of them, were not executions of divine decisions. God told Satan what *not* to do, but gave no positive command, or even definite suggestion. The "sovereignty" of God is not, I suggest, a very biblical idea, especially if one has a low opinion of the respect of sovereigns for the freedom of their subjects.

Value and Sympathy as the Keys to Power: The Final Mystery

How does God make things make themselves? Here at last we come to the final mystery. It is natural that it should be mysterious, for we are not divine. But still, we have some clues, without which we should have no right to any theology at all. How does the human mind, or sequence of experiences, influence the development, health, illness, and action of the human body, as it seems to do every moment? This, too, is mysterious, and many scientists have thought that we shall never understand it. Yet here also we have clues.

The open secret of the mind-body relation is this: *our cells respond to our feelings (and thoughts) because we respond to their feelings* (and would respond to their thoughts if they had any). Hurt my cells and you hurt me. Give my cells a healthy life, and they give me a feeling of vitality and at least minimal happiness. My sense of welfare tends to sum up theirs, and their misfortunes tend to become negative feelings of mine. I feel what many cells feel, integrating these feelings into a higher unity. I am somewhat as their deity, their fond heavenly companion. They gain their direction and sense of the goodness of life partly from intuiting my sense of that goodness, which *takes theirs intuitively into account.*

It comes to this: power over others, influence upon others, is either indirect (the power of one holding a loaded and cocked pistol, or with a large income) or it is direct and immediate. In the latter case the only explanation, I suggest, is that if X has an intrinsic value, say a sense of pleasure, to appropriate which is harmonizable with the life-style of Y and which therefore can enhance Y's feeling of value, then (if the spatio-temporal relations are favorable) X will tend to feel Y's value or feeling and will thus be influenced by Y. Somewhat indirectly, even brutal tyrants are partly influential by their intrinsic values, their charm, their feeling of confidence or exaltation, their flow of ideas, etc. *Intrinsic value gives power.*

Theologically applied, the principle explains the quality and scope of God's influence by the assumption that God appreciates and fully appropriates every feeling of value there is, sums up and integrates on the highest level possible what the creatures come to in value terms. As a result God charms every creature irresistibly to whatever extent is compatible with that creature's level of freedom. Plato and Aristotle hint at such an idea; but they did not realize that the highest intrinsic value must be the value of the most perfect and inclusive form of love. Because God loves each creature better than it or its fellows can love it, the creature, even though it is necessarily partly self-creative, cannot but make some response to the divine love. Thus Plato's analogy, in a form transcendent of Plato in certain respects, gives greater power to his theology than he himself could give it.

God's purpose is that there be happy creatures, that is, partly self-determined actualities. How can this purpose guarantee that some such actualities come into being? It is hardly an explanation to say that God's power is unlimited. However, consider what it would mean for there to be no response to the divine appeal. What would then make it true that God was in solitude, wholly without creatures to love or inspire? Would it be a mere nothing instead of a world, a mere emptiness? I hold, more explicitly and definitely than perhaps anyone before me has, that what makes a negative statement true is always something positive. "No food in the refrigerator" does not mean, and is not known to be true by observing, *nothing* in the refrigerator. We know it by observing the back wall of the interior or the shelves in a way that would not be possible were there solid or liquid foods on the shelves. Mere nothing plays no such role as that of making negative statements true. "Nothing" plays no role at all. Even a vacuum in the refrigerator would not be sheer nothing. So I hold that God would not know that there were no creatures by there being nothing instead. Indeed I question what sense it makes to suppose a supreme knower knowing its own knowing of its own knowing—of what?

The minimal idea seems to be of Creator-creature, not mere Creator or mere creature. However mysterious it seems, it must somehow be that the divine love and consequent divine charm is such that it can call into being creatures able to respond to this love (thus there is a "magical" aspect), even though the creatures come into being as partly self-active from the very start.

A version of the same mystery is, "What keeps the creative advance of the world going on, instead of petering out, so that, perhaps after the next moment, there would be nothing going on at all?" Well, no moment could make itself the last moment, for no such intrinsic character of a moment is conceivable. Would it be the nothing that followed the last moment? I do not find this intelligible. The divine-creaturely process can explain what needs explaining, which does not mean details causally deduced as necessary; for becoming is no deductive affair.

A merely creaturely or a merely divine process or reality explains nothing. The former has no principle of order, no directive to enable freedom to produce anything but meaningless chaos. The latter has no content; it is an empty power—to do what? Divinity is, for instance, infallible power to know whatever in particular could exist, and the certainty of knowing its existence be this existence a fact. But with only its own existence, what would the highest knower know? I see only a wholly verbal solution of this riddle. Without creatures, 'Father,' 'Son,' and 'Holy Ghost' are empty formulae—power-to-do without any doing. The love of the three for themselves and one another makes a verbal but empty answer to the question, "What is love when it has only three ideal forms, somehow equal yet genuinely differentiated, and there are no unideal forms at all?" God-with-creatures is the answer, not either side by itself. The Creator is eternally and necessarily creative, it is only the particular creatures whose very existence is contingent. Necessity and contingency are necessary to each other. But the necessity that there be some contingent things or other is entirely consistent with the genuine contingency of those things.

There is no logic requiring us to say, "That accidents happen, some accidents or other, is itself only an accident."

Contingency is not in the idea of contingency's having some real instances, but only in what instances. Contingency must be *somehow* actualized, but just *how* or *in just what* it is actualized: *that* is the contingency. No further contingency is required. In contrast, not only must there be something eternally necessary but the something necessary is eternally definite and has no alternative. The purely eternal and necessary aspect of deity could not have been otherwise than it is; it is necessarily all that it could have been. Since it could not have been prevented from existing, it is meaningless to call it unfortunate, bad, or in any sense open to criticism. In its empty abstract way it is absolutely perfect. Only the time-like aspect of the divine life is contingent—not that there could have failed to be some such aspect, but that the particular contents in which it is actualized could all have been otherwise. And their richness has no upper limit.

The main contention of this chapter, somewhat like that of the preceding one, is that it is an eighth theological mistake to regard belief in God as incompatible with the general idea of an evolution of species. Indeed, this is an understatement. Not only is the evolutionary idea of things partly making themselves and (in reasonable consequence) influencing their offspring or successors harmonious with, but something like it is derivable from, belief in God. Creaturely self-making or freedom is that without which the idea of God is scarcely a reasonable or beneficial one. Evolution is at least one way in which freedom of creatures can be given a basic role in a world view.

Psychicalism and Evolution

If there is a weakness in current evolutionary theory, it may derive, not from the admission of chance as pervasive, but from the tendency of science generally to limit itself to the supposedly merely physical, rather than psychical, aspects of reality. The "evolutionary naturalism" to which many philosophers and scientists incline is really a temporalized dualism. First, mere matter, without a trace of mind in any kind or degree, then (as "emergent" qualities of some physical wholes) the addition of primitive forms of mind, followed by more advanced forms.

With mind comes a distinctive kind of inheritance, additional to that carried by the genes, and it is this psychical inheritance which enables acquired characters to be passed on. For instance, most songbirds, to some extent at least, learn their songs partly by listening to their elders or contemporaries. Imitation of sounds comes in, and this involves psychological relations of stimulus-response and positive or negative reinforcement of modes of behavior. As new modes of behaving are discovered by individuals, some of these modes prove adaptive, and the individuals achieve thereby greater breeding success (say by nesting in barns rather than sites provided by nature before the coming of civilized human beings). Successive generations may learn this behavior from early experience, and thus the habits of an entire species may change considerably, especially with gregarious species like barn swallows.

One further step: physically inherited structures which happen to fit the new psychically inherited and adaptive modes will then also be adaptive and will be favored by natural selection. Thus indirectly even physical inheritance will eventually be altered by individual behavioral-psychical acquisitions. The farther down the evolutionary scale this factor can be supposed to go, the more power the theory can have to explain changes in species. Changes made by individuals in their behavior will not arise from mere random changes only but partly from the individuals' creative insights—in a word, intelligence, in however humble or primitive a form. But, as Dobzhansky says, the creativity here is that of individual creatures. They partly make, not only themselves, but their very species.

Creativity in creatures has both positive and negative aspects. It helps to produce new forms, and in the long run to enable animal life to fill the vast variety of niches in nature. If there are tree trunks, there will be animals seeking and finding food on tree trunks; if there is water, there will be animals living or (like penguins) at least feeding in water, etc. The result is what anyone who wants nature to be richly satisfying to contemplate must approve of: a vast variety of forms of life (and feeling), each internally harmonious and all capable of coexisting for long periods. And all these creatures may be supposed to enjoy their lives, to receive positive and negative reinforcements. (And, as Skinner says, the positive are the most constructive.) Creatures survive partly because they *want* to succeed in the little tasks inheritance assigns them and are at least slightly inventive in pursuing their short-run purposes. A bird may not know what a nest is for, but yet feel that a certain shape is satisfying in the arrangement of materials, and may try to bring about that shape. The option: either long-range purposes—like those of human beings after infancy or early childhood—or no purpose at all, is childish; but I am not convinced that all deniers of pervasive purpose in nature are adequately aware of how childish it is.

The Perils of a High Level of Mind and Freedom

The negative side of the psychical factor is that the greater the power of thinking becomes, the less behavior can be preprogrammed by physical inheritance (that is, by instinct), and the greater the individual variety in behavior. There is also greater danger that the individual will not perform its proper role in the ongoing of the species but will rather seek its own gratification and safety at the cost of its fellows and offspring. It may also exterminate other species symbiotically valuable to its own species. Hence religion is actually a biological necessity for a species on a sufficiently high level of intelligence. Bergson's explanation of primitive religion in these terms seems convincing. In thinking animals, religious sanctions must partly take the place of instinct as a check on species-destructive forms of behavior. Religious satisfactions or encouragements are also needed to counterbalance the fear aroused by the knowledge of mortality and the discontent arising from the knowledge of how probable it is that one's desires will meet with very limited success at best.

As science and philosophy grow more sophisticated and penetrating, primitive religion no longer satisfies those sharing in or aware of these inquiries. Commerce, communication, and travel acquaint us with the variety of religious, even on higher levels.

We see that they all make great claims, which cannot all be wholly true. We in this century, far more than our forebears, even in the Victorian period, are deep in the conflicts resulting from these factors. They are the penalties of intellectual and technological progress and have some tragic aspects.

Goethe, with his remarkable profundity, held that science has two rather different effects on culture. For scientists, especially the most creative ones, science brings inspiration, the vision of nature as mysteriously fascinating and beautiful, almost worthy of worship, although seemingly indifferent to human life and its problems. But to merely humanistically educated persons, science is chiefly destructive culturally. It destroys belief in fairy tales or myths and gives most people no comparably enjoyable views of reality to take their place. Goethe's fears on this head seem still relevant.

On many levels religions are struggling with the problem, or bundle of problems, just sketched. We all do what we can with the rival religious claims and solutions.

That the crimes and aimless hooliganisms in our society are partly caused by the lack of universally efficacious religious inspiration and guidance seems clear. It is not just that youngsters have insufficient religious motivation; their parents have lacked it, too, in many cases, and perhaps their grandparents. And these youngsters have been confronted with devastating, frustrating dilemmas, such as those connected with the Vietnam undertaking, or the nuclear danger now looming so threateningly, and the baffling rivalry of the great powers, brandishing weapons they dare not use, short of what looks like insanity, but also cannot see how to do away with.

I still do not believe that we should give up the scientific vision, with its majesty and beauty, or the philosophic-theological vision of cosmic mind as cosmic love.

An Ornithologist Who Opposed Evolution

About one aspect of the evolution controversy I happen to be something of an expert. This is the ornithological aspect. Wallace, who also discovered natural selection independently of Darwin—

like him, observing similar phenomena in tropical parts of the world (mostly different parts from those Darwin visited)—was, like Darwin, knowledgeable in ornithology. The agreement between these two superior Englishmen (superior in many notable respects) is impressive testimony to the strength of the case. It is stronger now. Unlike Darwin, Wallace maintained a religious faith to the end and did not admit that the origin of the human species was explicable in the same way as that of the other species. But in his time the fossil record of human and prehuman but human-like animals was far skimpier than it is now. When some rash religious critics of today say that we lack intermediate "links," they can only be saying that the gaps are greater than the theory implies they should be. But this is an extremely complex issue. Bones usually decay fairly rapidly; long preservation requires very special conditions; it is certain that we have not uncovered anything like all the fossils that lie somewhere buried in the earth. The gaps can only get smaller, and they are already small enough to convince any number of competent persons that the theory of "descent," as Darwin called it, is sound.

Returning to the ornithological aspect. We have a fossil bird intermediate between the dinosaurs and present-day birds, the archaeopteryx, which had feathers, the most universally distinctive feature of birds, but was far more like reptiles than are modern birds. A feathered lizard, 140 millions of years old, is a recent discovery. Considering how fragile bird bones are, the fossil record of the transition, many millions of years ago, from reptile to flying birds, may not be surprisingly scanty, assuming evolution.

During the several decades between Darwin's announcement (1858) of his theory and 1900, there was, in Gemany, first an enthusiastic reception of that theory, and then a fierce attack upon it. Bernard Altum (1824–1900), distinguished observer of birds and a Catholic priest, in his *Der Vogel und sein Leben* (*The Bird and Its Life*), argued vigorously and ingeniously against Darwinism.[2] If a strong case could have been made, this was the time and the man to make it. The negative case was more easily made then than now, for Lamarck's defence of inheritance of acquired characteristics had not been subjected to adequate tests, mutations were not known, no one had more than the vaguest idea of how the genetic machinery worked or what its laws were, fossil records were skimpy, etc. etc. But the religious motivation to try to refute Darwin was available and Altum had at least that. The nonevolutionary point of view was not held in the disrepute it is now; it would easily get a full hearing, and it did. In addition Altum was a vigorous thinker and a brilliant observer of birds. He gave a splendid account of the territorial theory of bird song, which he accepted. This was nearly sixty years before Eliot Howard's *Territory in Bird Life* quickly convinced the learned world of the validity of the theory. So far as I know, Altum was the last ornithologist of any marked distinction to take up the anti-evolutionary cause. For a time he made an impression. An unfortunate effect of his advocacy was that it prevented his admirable thought on territory from getting the attention it deserved.

Altum combined nearly all the mistakes one could well make, so far as evolution is concerned. Like Darwin he rejected the idea of chance, or of any freedom of the creatures, apart at least from human beings. A providential order meant for him the absolute exclusion of randomness or inharmony in nature. In the cosmic whole there was a place for everything and everything was in its place. Animals had no intelligence, even (he seems to imply) no feelings, and no purposes. Their actions were determined by the cosmos as a whole, a single integrated organism. How this related to Altum's theology I do not know. But it fits what I have been calling the tyrant idea of divine power. Animals are made by a higher power to do what they do.

Altum argues that the functions of song, for instance, are not in the least understood by the singing bird. Pure instinct *completely* determines the behavior. The nondivine purposive element is simply not there, in no matter how primitive a form. It follows that our species is essentially supernatural. Abruptly, with us, feeling, thought, and individual creativity come upon the scene. An unconscious, insentient, uninventive world suddenly—in our species alone— becomes conscious, emotional, and inventive. Or is it in all higher mammals? The evidence given for the lack of purpose in the other animals presupposes the view I have called childish, that what seems to do the work of purpose must be *either* the thoughtful, long-range, complex sort of thing that human language makes possible, *or* no purpose at all. The possibility of extremely simple, short-range purpose or desire, deficient in thought but not in mere feeling, is ignored. In this way the question of an evolution of feeling and the psychical generally is begged.

Altum is impressed, and rightly, by the aspects of symbiosis, living together, found in the relations of species. Insects and birds help plants to propagate, and plants help birds in various ways, and such things imply, he believes, a cosmic ordering to adjust species to one another. He does not distinguish, however, between, on the one hand, a basic ordering of partly free and self-ordering individuals, the cosmic aspect of the order being given by laws of nature that are not absolute in a more than statistical sense and, on the other hand, on ordering according to the classical idea of strictly sufficient reason leaving individuals no leeway for decision making. The latter is Altum's view. Only the cosmic power, expressed in instinct, effectively decides. "An animal does not act, but is acted upon." This as the reader knows is exactly the view I am combating in this book. It has, as one consequence, the nastiest form of the theological problem of evil, and, as another consequence, the problem of human freedom, and how, if we too have no freedom, we can form an idea of divine freedom, such as almost every theologian has claimed is part of the meaning of worship.

Has any present-day anti-evolutionist significant resources lacking to Altum? I fail to see it. On that side of the issue, Altum had everything of consequence that is available even now.

In my own book on birds, *Born to Sing: An Interpretation and World Survey of Bird Song*,[3] I take evolution for granted; but by stressing the psychical element, the creativity of the individual animal, and offering evidence for that in the case of singing birds, I do implicitly strengthen the evolutionary case. I give definite quantitative observational evidence for the territorial function, and consequent adaptive value, of song, and also and above all for the hypothesis that singing birds have a primitive form of what in us we call an aesthetic sense or musical feeling. Incidentally I confirm Altum's generalization: the gregariousness or sociality of a species is inversely correlated with its degree of song development. Singing is favored by an individualistic mode of existence, tending to separate widely in space the singer from its presumptive listener, whether mate or (sexual or territorial) rival. The principle is, the farther the song needs to be heard and distinguished from others audible at a given spot, the more distinctive it needs to be. Hence musical refinement and/or complexity are favored by nongregariousness. They are also favored by inconspicuousness in the normal habitat and with the normal behavior, on the principle that the more easily the bird can be identified visually the less it needs to be identified by sound.

Consider the geographical distribution of birds. In Madagascar many of the species are neither the same nor radically different from those some hundreds of miles away on the continent of Africa, and the explanation is at hand: the ancestors of the island birds came from the continent and in thousands or millions of years evolved into some new species. In the tropics this is easier by far to see than elsewhere, since in tropical regions, or those with mild winters, birds are mostly non-migratory and a moderate spatial separation tends to prevent interbreeding; hence new species may in time result. In the Galapagos Islands, which taught Darwin so much, the separation of one island from another enabled some finches, arriving no doubt at this or that island, to find their way in groups (finches tend to be gregarious), perhaps by a storm blowing birds out of their course, to other islands and so to develop many species to fit the various open niches on islands originally birdless. New Zealand has a similar relation to Australia as Madagascar has to Africa. Are we to look to the Book of Genesis for light on such situations? Without that document, we have a working method that really illuminates the facts (almost none of which are definitely referred to in that ancient writing).

Assume for a moment the nonevolutionary view: how then do we understand the fact that, on the hypothesis, what God has done is to make things such that observers of nature are bound, sooner or later, to be led to a conclusion which seems to wonderfully illuminate the phenomena; yet God has also made a certain Book, which, we are told, must be regarded as the infallible word of God, and which, we are also told, contradicts that conclusion. God's world and God's word seem remarkably incompatible. Why would

God so ingeniously deceive us? Is God "tempting" us, a suggestion that some actually propose?

We have navels. If Adam had one, then he came from a mother. At least this is the eminently reasonable conclusion. If not, then Adam was not fully human as we know our species. The point goes much farther. Each of us is unconsciously influenced (who doubts it?) by having spent months in a womb and by having been born more or less painfully into a very different environment. If Adam lacked these experiences, how different he would be from us as well as from any other mammal! One could go on and on. The human fetus goes through stages which to some extent mimic structures in what evolutionists view as our remote ancestors. Here again, the Creator seems determined to deceive us, to trick us into becoming evolutionists.

Perhaps, after all, creation science ought to be taught in school, it is so rich in farcical aspects from the evolutionary standpoint. Who could be bored if full justice were done to that aspect? And yet, alas, the thing we are asked to take seriously is more pathetic and sad than amusing. It shows how much some natures crave easy answers, definite slogans with which to encourage friends and intimidate enemies—or offspring. I received yesterday a circular from a woman in Canada who dares to speak of her "knowing as God knows" all sorts of definite truths which she can easily put into words, such as that the words of the Bible took fully into account everything that has happened since the words were written down (the view of omniscience that the Socinians rejected for carefully considered reasons). Ah, well . . .

We human beings, naked apes, featherless bipeds, who enjoy the privileges of conscious thought, must also bear its burdens. The other animals may in their way be closer to sublime wisdom than we sometimes are. *They* live their roles in the divinely-inspired, partly self-realized Scheme; we may, much of the time, be living in some little scheme of our own imagining.

The writers of The Book were, I dare say, hardly fundamentalists. Certainly *they* did not drive in cars and use electronic machinery, as some of their modern readers do, devoid of any inkling of the scientific spirit, the "natural piety," which made these inventions possible. None of *them* exhibited even a suspicion of the evolutionary biology which, centuries later, convinced most relevantly educated people by its picture of the origin of our and all species, or of the physics and astronomy which penetrated to the ultramicroscopic atoms and explored the development of the solar system and star galaxies.

Has someone begun to tell us about "creation physics"? Would that be very different from just physics, plus an attempt to conceive a theological interpretation? Such an interpretation need not be an account of how our present cosmos sprang complete from the disembodied mind of deity; it might rather tell how the divine Mind incarnated itself in some initial stage of the development of that cosmos (the beginning of our "cosmic epoch," in Whitehead's phrase) governed by divinely decided laws which leave the details of happenings to decisions made by countless kinds of nondivine creatures. What came before that cosmic epoch may perhaps be beyond both physics and theology to discover. If divine awareness is in principle exalted above the human, there must be some truths which only the former can know.

The authors of the biblical writings show no realization of how science and technology, with their tendency toward increasingly rapid accumulation of skills, might someday so drastically alter the death and birth rates, especially of infants and women, and in addition so reduce the importance of brute physical strength, as to quite change the place of women in society and put into permanent question the overwhelming male dominance that had hitherto characterized human groups. Biblical literalists ask us to pretend that this is to make no difference in how we react, for instance, to Paul's instructions about how to treat women. Yet these same literalists are themselves ignoring some other biblical injunctions which also, obviously, no longer apply. They tell us that one cannot draw the line between texts to be taken seriously and texts not to be taken seriously. But in practice they do draw this line. Would they really like to put homosexuals to death (Leviticus) if only our laws allowed it?

How easily our built-in "thinking machines," our brains (which are also far more than thinking machines, but are at least that, or something like that) can make slips in deriving conclusions from assumptions, or err in adopting assumptions! Instincts, tested through thousands of years, are much more reliable as far as they go. But highly inventive, thinking creatures produce new problems and must invent new solutions.

In speaking of the wisdom of the other animals, I have in mind that we cannot understand God as having simply our kind of thinking consciousness to the nth degree. God does not have some tiny field of direct and distinct (in creatures it is only relatively distinct) acquaintance with reality (perception) and know the rest by brilliant inferences from this small sample and recollections of other samples. God's field of distinct perception is the de facto whole itself. No thinking is thus needed to get to the whole from the part. God's intelligence is not, as ours is, "discursive," as the older thinkers expressed it. To form the conception of God we have to try to understand what function is left for thought when perception does the entire job of yielding the physical whole.

It is remarkable (but one can explain it) that, while classical theologians wrote about the "will" and "knowledge" of God, the word *"perception"* was usually avoided in this context. Whitehead is original here, too, for he attributes "physical prehensions," equivalent to perceptions, to deity. But then, what need is there for divine thinking? The answer seems to be that, because the future is only potential, a matter of more or less universal "might-be's, would-be's, and must-be's" (in Peirce's terms) rather than fully concrete or particularized actualities, God must have awareness of what we call universals, and the awareness of the universal is what concepts give us. In this way God can be supposed to distinguish our fragmented awareness of the physical whole of things from His-Her unfragmented awareness. *We* have to treat the distant and not-perceived through concepts of what *might* be out there beyond our field of vision, hearing, and smelling. *We* use universals or concepts in a way God would not have to. But God has to be aware of the truth involved in concepts, since that is *the* truth so far as the uncreated future is concerned. And so, too, God knows mathematical truths, which concern universals, abstract possibilities.

God is like the other animals, rather than like us, in the following way: for the other animals, the field of perception is almost the whole, so far as the animal has definite awareness of that whole. The animal's instincts take the real whole into account to some extent; but of this the animal is largely unconscious. It does little thinking about what is not at the moment perceived, unless it has in the very near past been perceived. So, for the animal, the animal's body and its near environment almost are the whole. For God there is no external environment, the divine body just is the spatial whole; moreover, this body is vividly and distinctly perceived. For most animals, the near external environment is almost the entire relevant environment. In addition, the reliability of instinct has some analogy to that of divine wisdom. It is our kind of animal alone that would win the prizes in a contest for extremes of folly—knights tilting at windmills, sinners trembling at visions of hell fire. So Plato's description of the world as patterned after "the ideal animal," or the ideal of animality, makes some sense.

I once spent perhaps half an hour with a German psychoanalyst who had studied under Freud. He surprised me by saying that he believed in God, and that we were related to God as our cells are to us. Naturally, I was pleased by this information.

For God, too, reality *develops*, and for God, as for us, the end is not yet. Indeed, though there may be an end to our cosmos, as well as our species, there can be no end of the divine-creaturely process, out of which even laws are born.

Theologians used to object to the idea that "the world" is "coeternal with God," making it seem that God's eternity has a rival. But this is to misunderstand the import of "the world." If it means the present system of natural laws, there is no need to take that as eternal. If other laws are conceivable, God is not to be forbidden by us to make use eventually of these other possibilities for patterning a universe. That God with no world is probably an absurd idea does not mean that there is a definite individual which is not God and is eternal. The world consists of individuals, but the totality of individuals as a physical or spatial whole is God's body, the Soul of which is God. So there is no eternal, worldly individual, rival to God. Simply, eternally God has some creaturely individuals or other—indeed, taking the divine past into account, an infinity of them, but a growing infinity, in the meaning that Bertrand Russell at least held is not a contradiction. So, in a sense, even God evolves, but in a decidedly transcendent or divine sense.

Notes

1. Emerson wrote these still pertinent words in his Journal in March, 1843. See *The Heart of Emerson's Journals*, ed. Bliss Perry (Boston: Houghton Mifflin Co., 1909, 1926), pp. 196f.

2. For Altum's importance, see Erwin Stresemann, *Ornithology: From Aristotle to the Present* (Cambridge, Mass., and London: Harvard University Press, 1975), pp. 328–30, 215, 238, 273, 322, 341, 360, 361.

3. *Born to Sing: An Interpretation and World Survey of Bird Song* (Bloomington: University of Indiana Press, 1973).

Chapter 4
Equal Love for Self and Other,
All-Love for the All-Loving

The Moral Argument against Heaven and Hell

I N THIS CHAPTER the ethical aspects of classical theology and its newly worked out alternative are to be considered. The traditional idea (though not the one that prevails in the Old Testament) is that good behavior in this life must be motivated by concern for one's welfare after death. People, it was thought, are not to be trusted to love their neighbors in this life unless they have something for themselves to hope for or fear after they die. We are to gamble with God about rewards or punishments in a later life earned by how we respond to divine commands in this life. How much sin can we commit and still, upon dying, find ourselves, if not in heaven, then at least not in hell but in purgatory? Berdyaev called this Dantesque scheme "the most disgusting morality ever conceived." If it were possible to startle those—millions, presumably—who still today accept this scheme, Berdyaev's words ought to do it. But probably it is not possible. James Joyce, in an early novel, expressed an attitude somewhat similar to Berdyaev's. Joyce also wrote a limerick to make the point, which ends: ". . . the smell / Of a horrible hell / That a Hottentot wouldn't believe in." (I owe this information to my learned friend Robert Palter.)

A more gentle response than Berdyaev's to the idea of rewards and punishments after death can be read in a pleasantly readable mystery story by a contemporary Jewish writer:

"I'd like to ask the rabbi what he meant when he said that punishment and reward after death deprived man of free will?"

The rabbi paused and said, "Well, I suppose it depends on what you mean by free will."

"Why freedom of choice, of course. The right to choose—"

"Between bread and toast?" the rabbi challenged. "Between turning right or left at a crossing? The lower animals have that kind of free will. For man, free will means the freedom to choose to do something he knows is wrong, wicked, evil, for some immediate material advantage. But that calls for a fair chance of not being discovered and punished. Would anyone steal if he were surrounded by policemen and certain of arrest and punishment? And on the other hand, what virtue is there in a good deed if the reward is certain? Since God is presumably all-seeing and all-knowing, no transgression goes undetected, and no good deed fails to be noted. So what kind of free will is that? How does it differ from the free will of the laboratory rat that is rewarded by food if he goes down one path of a maze and is given an electric shock if he goes down another?"

"Then what happens after death according to your people?"

"We don't pretend to know."[1]

This is one way of spelling out what Berdyaev meant.

It is a conviction of mine that a test of antisemitism is in the way one answers the question: "Can I take seriously the idea that it just might be that the Jews, in their differences from Christians, have been more right all along on some issues?" If the answer is "Yes," then perhaps there is no antisemitism. If "No," then I have my suspicions. (I am in no sense whatever Jewish.)

Is it really necessary, in order to induce good behavior in people, to convince them that they will be rewarded or punished after death for the way they have lived? The ancient Jews did not think so. Many modern Jews do not. Is Jewish behavior less law-abiding than gentile behavior, are Jews the murderers and thieves in our society? The abusers of wives or of children? I am not aware that this is so. How about Japan, where Christians are a tiny minority? There the religious picture is complex and subtle; but we know that the Japanese population has a vastly smaller proportion than ours of those who kill or rob others. I suspect in fact that the Japanese are today surpassed by no other people and equaled by few in their good behavior, as judged by fairly reasonable standards (other than the admitted fact that male chauvinism is still rather marked in them). Yet I doubt if you could show that hopes of heaven or fears of hell loom very large in that country, granting that one branch of Japanese Buddhism does have recognizable duplicates of the Western ideas of heaven and hell.

How well did the heaven and hell idea ever work in influencing behavior? Frank Knight, the philosophical economist of the mid-century, once said that the relation between religious beliefs and behavior is "one of the deepest sociological mysteries." There is some influence, but it is hard to pin down factually. In any case the unfreedom of behavior controlled by threats and promises, the reliance on naked self-interest, is repellent once one sees it for what it is, a confession of disbelief in love as the principle of principles, and a glorification of egocentricity. If to be good is to be loving, how can we motivate good behavior by rewards and threats? What have they to do with love of neighbors? If we love people we want to help them. How can doing what we want to do require a reward, beyond the satisfaction of having a rational aim and capacity to realize it? Unless being loving is its own reward it is not really loving.

Abortion and the Nonabsoluteness of Personal Identity

In a previous chapter (chapter 2, section B) I remarked that it is clearly false to say that a fetus, infant, or child is strictly identical with an adult, even though the adult grew out of the child. It is also clearly false to say, as "pro-lifers" seem to say, or imply, that because the fetus or infant came from two persons and can (with much help from persons) grow into a person, therefore, it already is a person. The fallacy tries to hide under the vague terms 'life' and 'human': "When does human life begin?" As I write this, the president of this country, in a public address, implies that if the human fetus is alive abortion must be prohibited. But the ethical and legal question is, "When does an individual human animal become a person in the full sense?" For it is persons who are more valuable, intrinsically of a higher order, than mere animals. And persons are more valuable because they think on a level of which even the chimpanzees are, so far as we know, incapable. The Greek word *'logos'* (*'word,'* also, *'reason')* points to this distinctiveness of the human being as such. There is zero evidence that any newborn infant reasons in any sense beyond or equal to the capacity of dogs, apes, or porpoises.

In order to justify strongly qualifying any legal or moral right to put an end to so important a natural process as a human pregnancy, it is not necessary to deny or attempt to conceal plain facts such as those just cited. It is not a mere opinion that *there are enormous (I am using words carefully) differences between a fetus and an adult human being, differences that are similar to those by which we judge ourselves to be more valuable than even the apes.* To argue on the assumption that these differences are irrelevant to the question of abortion is to beg that question so patently and grossly that it is somewhat hard to believe in the good faith of those who do this. And the "pro-life" literature is full of such question-begging.

I give an extreme example to illustrate this. Jesus said, "Suffer little children to come unto me, for of such is the Kingdom of Heaven." This has actually been quoted to imply that Jesus meant, "Suffer even little fetuses to come unto me." Not only did Jesus not say or reasonably mean that, he did not even say or mean, "Suffer infants to come unto me." At any rate, it is a wild guess to suppose that he meant that. A child such as Jesus had before him, showing fondness for him, was much more than a newborn infant. It was beginning to show the unique human power of speech and to enjoy personal relations in a manner beyond the nonhuman creatures. Physiologists know that its brain cells must have been matured definitely beyond the state of the newly born, or of a fetus, which some physiologist has compared to the brain cells of a pig. Yet "pro-lifers" like to appeal to science to support their contentions. Of course the fetus is alive! So are puppies and kittens. Of course it is human (who ever in this controversy has denied this?) if "human" here means that its origin is in the union, in a human womb, of a human sperm and a human egg cell. To pretend that this settles the question of value is to grossly beg the question.

The aliveness and humanity of a fetus, meaning its origin in, and (given sufficient help) likely development into, human adulthood is admitted by all parties. The question, however, concerns, not the value of the origin, or the possible eventual stage of develoment, of the fetus, but the value of the actual stage. Not everything that can be is, and the "equal value of the actual and the possible" is not an axiom that anybody lives by or could live by. Many things in an early stage of development would have an importance in a later stage which they lack in their earliest stages. In nearly every society until recent centuries it was taken for granted that killing of human adults is a vastly more serious matter than even infanticide (if the latter is done by the parent or parents). This is enough to show that the idea of a fetus as a person in the full sense is not so plainly true that it can be used as a noncontroversial premise for political or moral conclusions. Nor is there anything in the Constitution to justify it. Did the makers of that Constitution— who brought themselves to make partial exception of women and blacks and even, in some respects, of half-grown children, all of whom, beyond controversy, have the unique human capacities of fluent speech and reasoning which no fetus has and which alone justify, if they do, killing other animals for food—did these men have fetuses in mind when they wrote about the rights of persons or citizens? To equate treatment of women or blacks with treatment of fetuses is a gross insult to members of those two groups of undoubted persons.

If being a typical member of the Kingdom of Heaven were really like being a fetus, the saying of Jesus would scarcely be an appealing—if even an intelligible—invitation to membership in that Kingdom.

Would it not be well if some of the rhetorical tears shed over the dying of fetuses were saved for the tragic sufferings, in many cases the deep misery, of women, many of them very young, who against their intentions and wishes, have become pregnant? Their unwillingness to be mothers may have various grounds, by no means necessarily selfish or unreasonable. We are in a society that does a miserable job of teaching the truth about sex, also about love and friendship. Parents with the courage, tact, and knowledge to impart that truth effectively are apparently uncommon; and yet some of the others, one surmises, are the very ones who wish to prevent schools from doing what they themselves cannot or will not do.

We should all be "for life," especially for the lives of those who quite certainly are persons. Unless that is given a *clear priority*, the whole pro-personal-life idea looks like a contradiction. And that contradiction is to be put into the Constitution—or the law of the land?! On the chance that what seems to most of us, and has seemed to most societies, to be far from a person is really a person, one is to demand that what we all agree is a person is to have *at most* only equal claims. So weak is human judgment in many among us that it can offer such a proposal seriously.

It is only too true that birth control, and the availability of abortion when the former fails (and only abstinence is infallible), may encourage some to live frivolously and miss the very real values that fidelity to a single mate can give. I have had fifty-four years of experiencing these values. I have not sought or accepted sexual relationships on any other basis. I do not need to be told what many are missing by following a different life-style. But in old-fashioned civilized societies there have always been many who also missed them. These are very difficult problems. I wish I knew all the answers to the relevant questions. But I think I know that some of the most emphatic pronouncements come from those who do not know the anwsers. They want to take a sad situation, huge numbers of women, many still little more than children, pregnant at the wrong time and in the wrong way, and make it even worse. If the Supreme Court is our last bastion against their endeavors, then how fortunate we are that the court exists!

The resourcefulness of one-issue fanatics in obscuring issues is almost inexhaustible. Consider the endlessly reiterated adjective "innocent" used of fetuses. If, and only if, the defenders of a right to abort (in certain cases) had ever used, or were likely ever to use, as argument the contention that fetuses are wicked and ought to be *punished*, only then would the innocence of the fetus be a relevant consideration. Of course the assumption is totally false and therefore the consideration as used is irrelevant.

The innocence of the fetus is indeed somewhat relevant if used on the other side of the argument. The fetal innocence is like the innocence of the other animals, a total incapacity to distinguish right from wrong and therefore to be wicked. This supports the view that in value qualities the fetus is drastically inferior to a person (normally and responsibly so-called).

Another irrelevant yet actually used argument is to ask the defender, not of abortion but of a limited right to abort, how would you have liked it if your mother had decided to abort *you* in the early fetus stage so that you would never have enjoyed the career you have enjoyed or any out-of-the-womb career? The answer is that, using pronouns responsibly, *I* would neither have liked nor disliked this, for there simply would not have been what "I" refers to when the author of this book employs the word. In an early-stage fetus there is no conscious selfhood, much less, if possible, than there is in a gibbon ape. Ask any psychologist.

The term "pro-life" seems to imply (another red herring) that those who grant a limited right to abortions are against "life." It is a statistical fact that properly done abortions in early fetus stages are far safer for the mother than ordinary childbirth. Even this fact seems to get pushed under the rug. It may not be decisive but it is relevant. Moreover, it does not begin to exhaust the ways in which the "pro-life" politicians are cheerfully endangering the lives of undoubted persons. By putting many very personal matters into the hands of the police and magistrates, they may greatly increase the number of badly done abortions, and do harm to members of families in which an additional birth may be a catastrophe. I could go on.

To attempt to legislate a total cessation of abortions comes close to threatening civil war. What consensus there is concerning the topic is strongly against such legislation. It would be a classic case of bad lawmaking. The controversy is also a classic case of the way we human beings can be entangled in our own language and by verbal ambiguities deceive one another and, above all, ourselves, unless by good luck and good will we have been taught and have learned how to use words responsibly. We are all only too likely to take advantage of such ambiguities when so doing promises to increase our political power. And the "pro-life" movement is definitely political. It is quite other than a group of saints acting out their saintliness.

Identity, Nonidentity, and the Primacy of Love

Our concern here is only incidentally with abortion, important in a practical way as that subject is. Our concern with the meaning of personal identity, however, is far more than incidental. I hold that every major mistake about God involves a mistake about human nature, and (generally speaking) vice versa. And I regard it as a fact about the history of religions that only one of the great religions has been at all clear and correct about the sense in which a person is the same reality through change. This religion is not Christianity, which until very recently has, in its philosophy, nearly always analyzed personal identity partly wrongly. It has supposed that a person is simply one reality from birth (or before) until death (or after), although this one reality has partly different (indeed very different) qualities at different times. Various logicians and a few philosophers in the West have pointed out the confusion in this account (H. Scholz in Germany, Bertrand Russell in England, Carnap, Whitehead, and William James in this country, David Hume long ago in England), but philosophers and theologians have tended to ignore or weakly answer their criticisms. The example of Aristotle has been somewhat unhelpful in this regard. As with a good many other questions, Plato's philosophy, carefully considered, tends to correct Aristotle's mistake, but Aristotle came later and his wonderfully versatile genius gave him enormous influence. His "substances" still stroll the world.

A Spanish philosopher of our time, Julián Marías, has pointed to the truth by saying: "A person [probably Marías did not have fetuses or infants in mind] is the same person through change, but not the same thing." Or, as I said above, with each change we have a new concrete reality, not simply the identical reality with new qualities. There is numerical, not merely qualitative, alteration. That John Smith (born of parents A and B at time *t*) is "the same person" day after day and year after year means that John Smith does not become Henry Jones (born of two parents other than A and B or at another time than *t*) nor does John Smith become an elephant or a mountain or (after infancy) anything other than a human person through the changes in question. But John Smith on Monday and John Smith on Tuesday are two realities, numerically as well as qualitatively distinguished. This, I submit, is plain fact. The two are in different loci in space-time, they are concrete realities that can be or have been observed as such. What is not fully concrete is the "identity" of the two. This is the abstraction that both are human persons and that between the two was a series of intermediaries, with no definitely observable break between them. Thus the one reality "turned into" the other. None of this is clearly and correctly stated by saying that the two are simply identical. Identity in the strict sense first defined by Leibniz means: with all properties the same. With strict identity, differences are not in what is referred to but only in the referring expressions. Genetic identity, as of persons, is a nonstrict identity. By insisting on treating the facts otherwise, one is, knowingly or not, playing fast and loose with language; and it is foolish to suppose that this can be done in a serious and difficult question of religion, ethics, or metaphysics without misleading others and/or oneself.

A nonstrict identity is one in which there are two or more concrete actualities with partly differing qualities. The actualities may be *partly* identical. For instance, A may include B, which is then strictly identical with a part or constituent of A but not with A as a whole. There is a case for the view that a person in a later state includes that person in an earlier state, though not vice versa. So far as memory is involved, A-now includes A-then, for A-now-remembering-A-then is not complete without A-then. This is the Bergson-Whitehead doctrine that memory is somehow literal embracing of the past in the present. In whatever sense this is correct, there is genuine—though only partial and nonstrict, yet numerical—identity of a person through change. Only I remember my very past in the inward way in which I remember it. I remember it mostly vaguely and partially, but still I-now cannot be fully described without mentioning that past of mine. So genetic personal identity is not mere similarity plus the mere continuity of Hume's or Russell's analysis (and some Buddhist analyses) of genetic identity. They overstated the nonstrictness of genetic identity. But this does not justify pretending that it is really strict identity. It is, in many glaringly obvious ways, very far from that. For instance, in deep sleep one is not even a conscious individual. One's body is there, but where are one's thoughts or feelings? If this is a small difference, what is a large one? It is like the general difference between a tree and a higher animal. In fact, Aristotle well said, "A tree is like a man sleeping [and not dreaming] who never wakes up."

The importance of the distinction between complete or strict and only partial identity is seen when we take into account that it is not only in memory that we seem to have the past in the present. This happens in perception also. Events we see happening actually happened before we saw them—long before, if the happenings were far off in the starry sky. It is arguable, and I believe true, that no account of the present is complete without referring to past events as perceptually embraced in that present. If this is so, then I-now may be partly identical with you as a moment ago. Coming closer still to the heart of the problem, if I-now feels a physical pain, then I-now embraces intuitively what is either just now happening, or has just already happened, in some of my cells. There are reasons for preferring the second interpretation. But either way I am partly identical with those cells, and with perceived neighbors, and not merely with my previous remembered states of consciousness.

We are now ready to look at the theological and ethical importance of our analysis of genetic identity. The great preacher of love or "charity," Paul, wrote, "We are members one of another." I once (in a class taught by Rufus Jones at Haverford College) had my life changed by this text, plus the philosopher Royce's discussion of it as llustrative of what he called "community." It started me on a path that led far beyond Royce's own philosophy and also beyond classical theology. Paul was right, in a reasonable sense literally right, in the text quoted. And his eloquent poem in praise of "charity" or love shows how wonderfully he knew the religious significance of his words. But still he stopped short of full understanding.

What Jesus termed "the law and the prophets," in other words, the essentials of religious ethics, were the two "great commandments": love God with all your being (heart, mind, strength) and your neighbor *as* yourself. It is not said, "*nearly* as yourself." Love for self and the other are in principle to be on the same footing; the ideal is their strict *equality*. How few are the Western philosophers or theologians who have really accepted this proposition!

Nearly all have tended to say, love your neighbor because that is the way to promote your own future welfare, if not in this life then in the next. The justification of altruism was sought in enlightened self-interest. Self-interest, however, was taken as its own justification. Self-love stands on its own feet, but love of others is indirect self-love. I submit, this betrays the Gospel ideal. And it does this in two ways.

If personal identity is strict or unqualified, is the nonidentity *between* persons similarly unqualified, so that "We are members one of another" is simply false? How can A love B as A loves A, if the point of "A loves A" is that A simply is A, whereas B is simply not A? Sheer identity is to explain the one love, sheer nonidentity to explain the other love. What can the two loves have in common? How can they be equals? This is one way in which the traditional interpretation of "person" betrays the Gospel ideal.

The other way is equally manifest. We are told that love for God is to be the all-in-all of our motivation. This contradicts the idea that self-love needs no justification, stands on its own feet as entirely rational in itself. On the contrary, it stands under the strict injunction that it is to count for nothing except as it is somehow included in love for God, which love is to be the inclusive motivation. We are to love ourselves as valuable to God. This is *exactly* how we are to love the neighbor. "Inasmuch as ye have done it to the least of these, ye have done it unto me." The justification for love of others is as direct as that for love of self. The only detour (if it is that) is to bring in God, and it is the same for self-love. Thus the two great commandments, properly understood, are entirely in harmony with each other, and neither is in harmony with the traditional Western doctrine of motivation.

After Rufus Jones, the philosophical mystic of the Society of Friends, had started me on the consideration of the meaning of Christian or Judaeo-Christian love, I began to move toward a view which differed somewhat both from classical and from Royce's theology, but which, I gradually discovered, had some elements in common, not only with various modern or recent Western philosophies, but also with some views of ancient and modern Buddhism.

It is Buddhists who really went the limit in qualifying personal identity to allow for partial identity with others. This was called the 'no soul, no substance' doctrine. They really believed that we are members one of another. Personal identity, personal nonidentity, are alike partial. There is no absolute and direct justification for self-love in contrast to a merely roundabout one for love of others. Both are on much the same footing and neither makes much sense merely by itself. Apart from our interest in others, what are we? Start with those others that are our bodily cells, and go on to our sympathy with characters in history and fiction, our love for relatives and friends, other lesser animals, plants. Apart from all this, we have no self. It is our loves that make us anything worth mentioning. In a generalized sense of the word, it is "altruism" that explains self-love, not the other way. I-now sympathizes with my probable future and remembered past selves, and that is my self-love. It is no mere identity. And I, as ordinary language puts it, (partially) "identify myself with," "sympathize with," other people's past and future selves. Sympathy, the root of altruism, is the common principle of all love and all senses of identity as applied to individuals.

What the Buddhists chiefly lacked, though in some sects they came close to it, was an idea of God adequate to express their insight into human motivation. In this, the West, at long last, did them one better—after nearly two thousand years of wandering in the wilderness of an extreme pluralism of persons and other "substances," each perfectly self-identical and perfectly nonidentical with one another. Similarly, God was a supreme person or substance, in a quasi-absolute fashion nonidentical with the creatures. Gradually, with increasing clarity, in various parts of the world, a new way of qualifying the plurality of persons, things, and God, capable of interpreting the belief in the ultimacy of love, is being worked out. A branch of Hinduism has for several centuries represented some such view (the Bengali school, founded by Sri Jiva Goswami); Whitehead and other process theologians, Cobb, Ogden, and others are recent or contemporary Western examples. This view has had representatives or enthusiasts in many branches of Christianity, some in Judaism, and at least one (Iqbal) in Islam.

If we reject the Buddhist-Whiteheadian view (that a human career, for example, is not a strictly single reality with differing qualities but an apparently continuous *succession* of realities each as a whole new), then we are not only supposing that for over twenty centuries the Buddhists, who thought with care about the matter all this time, were simply mistaken, but we are also supposing that Hume, Russell, a number of accomplished logicians besides Russell and Whitehead (one of whom, Scholz, was a trained theologian who wrote a fine book on Christian love)—and, besides all this, that even contemporary physicists, who keep telling us that they have been forced to the conclusion that reality consists of "events not things" (meaning self-identical yet changing things)—are also in this simply mistaken. You can suppose all this, but still, what consensus could be more impressive than that between one of the great religious traditions, much modern philosophy, and the most exact natural science? We shall see in the next section that the biblical doctrine of divine love is most readily interpretable in the Buddhist-Whiteheadian way.

It does not help here to appeal to ordinary language. The assertion of strict or complete rather than partial identity is not a piece of ordinary language. It is a highly technical, but as such manifestly paradoxical, assertion. Ordinary uses of pronouns and proper nouns are quite consistent with the theory of only-partial identity with self and only-partial nonidentity with others.

Self-Identity as Attribute of God

If, in ordinary cases, the identity of an individual through change is a highly qualified or relative matter, and if God, as maintained in Chapter 1, is to be conceived as in some respect changeable, then is the identity of Deity analogously qualified or relative? I answer, Yes—but, as with all analogies, and especially the one between a creature as such, or the human being as such, and God— there is difference as well as similarity. It is easy to see that the relativity involved in the passage from unconsciousness in dreamless sleep to waking consciousness, or between nonrational infantilism and adult rationality, or vicious hatred and kindly love, are not to be attributed to Deity. Indeed, God must have something almost like the strict identity many seem to think they find in each of us. The divine **integrity** through change must be ideally perfect. Divine action as righteous, principled, or loving must be infallibly constant. The only change must be in *increase* in whatever aspects of value are incapable of an absolute maximum, these being summed up in the idea of enjoying the beauty, the aesthetic harmony and richness, of creation. Only in this aspect is there any "shadow of turning" in God.

There is also the question of the relativity of nonidentity with others as applied to Deity. Are we and God members one of another? Again the answer is, Yes, but with a difference in principle in this supreme case, as contrasted to ordinary ones. Deity is the highest possible form of the inclusion of others in the self and the highest possible form of the self being included in others. Infallibly and with unrivaled adequacy aware of all others, God includes others—not, as we do, in a mostly indistinct or largely unconscious manner, but with full clarity and consciousness. Another statement of Paul's is relevant here too: "In God we live and move and have our being." Since God forgets nothing, loses no value once acquired, our entire worth is imperishable in the divine life. This is the Whiteheadian "objective immortality in the consequent nature of God." It is the non-Pauline version of "O death, where is thy sting?" Also God, being ubiquitous, universally relevant to all creatures, is present to every creature, included in it in whatever manner the nature of the particular creature is capable of experiencing God, in most cases without anything like distinct consciousness. In this extremely generalized sense, God is *universal object as well as universal subject.* No creature is universal in either role.

The Present Condition of Humankind

In a world—that is to say, on a planet—of fear and violence (which now seems potentially unlimited), what can a religion of universal love contribute? It can at least relieve us of fears of evils which, so far as real knowledge goes, are imaginary, such as the fear of a God who loves creatures so little as to threaten them with some supernatural hell. After Hiroshima we know that there can be hell enough on earth. Such a God would love us, not for what we are, unusually complex and unusually free and conscious animals with limited life spans, but for what there is no clear evidence we are, creatures with supernatural, unending careers, only a vanishingly small fraction of which are to be lived on earth.

A religion of love can encourage us to look upon nature as a realm of love and freedom, whose members, in an extended sense fellow creatures, are in their humbler way also "images of God," testaments to the divine nature. Thus it can express and enlighten the current concern for the environment as no mere platform for our strutting about, or set of exploitable resources for our survival and luxurious living, but rather as a vast system of embodiments of and suitable objects for sympathetic participation. We thus become citizens of the universal society, the old Stoic idea, but without the Stoic reduction of freedom to mere preprogrammed voluntariness.

It is important to realize that some of our current problems are radically different from those which confronted our species in the days of the founding of the major religions and that the differences result chiefly from science, pure and applied. We can either try to content ourselves with applied science (technology), refusing to open our minds to the essential spirit of science, the most intensive, constructive, cooperative form of curiosity about the concrete world around us, or we can open our minds to that spirit. We cannot do this while holding tenaciously to the letter of religious texts as definitive in all the matters with which, taking their words at face value, they seem to deal. In science no book settles once for all what is to be believed. The God whose "images" we are is supremely intelligent and (we may presume) bids us be intelligent, is supremely creative or free and bids us be creative and free in our own appropriate ways. Science is a principal form of this creativity. It is really an intellectual form of love, a search for the hidden beauties of nature which are expressions of and contributions to the supreme Artist and Appreciator of art. Scientists, especially the greatest among them, have often used the word 'beauty,' and often, too, the word 'God,' to communicate their feelings about their work.

If the religion of love, freedom, and beauty cannot be content with traditional theology in those aspects of it which are criticized in this book, it also cannot be content with a merely atheistic or materialistic view. We have no reason to be uncritically impressed by present-day China or Russia. The consequences of a world-view blind to the great "sun" of love (the concern of life for life, experience for experience, feeling for feeling, consciousness for consciousness, freedom for freedom) are not hard to see in the dark sides of communist activities. But this does not mean that we must substitute mere fear or hatred for the sense that communists, too, are our human fellows, as are the literal-minded traditionalists in religion. All are expressions of and contributions to the divine life. And our society, too, has its dark side. Both great powers threaten humankind.

A Requirement for Ethical Judgments

On one point there might be a rather general consensus among theologians and philosophers: Any ethical judgment should be capable of defence without telling falsehoods, misstating facts, arguing from ambiguity, or playing fast and loose with language. The "pro-life" literature is mostly a string of verbally implied identifications of fertilized egg cell with fetus, of fetus with infant, infant with child, child with youth, youth with adult. I repeat, any cause is suspect which ignores or denies distinctions so great as that between even a child and an animal form (say a three- or four-month-old fetus) in actual functioning far below the higher mammalian level, or which collapses the contrast between 'actually valuable' and 'potentially valuable,' as though 'capable of becoming such and such' were no different from 'actually being such and such.'

A child speaking with some fluency, say three years old, is already, for all we yet know, beyond the mental level even of an ape. But a fetus or newborn infant is well below that level. And a two-month-old fetus is vastly below it. Indeed, this is, as differences in the world go, one of the really great ones. Our lives are *enormous* journeys from less than nothing of rational personhood to the fullness of personhood. It is one of the wonders of the world that this journey is possible. But the journey is the progressive *creation* of value, with no fixed value there from the start.

Suppose the fetus really is the beginning of an endless career and hence infinitely important. Its destruction cannot, on the hypothesis, cut short that career, and might for all we know go on better in the supposed supernatural state after death. Thus the infinitizing of human lives is of no help in determining how their finite careers on earth are to be viewed. Rather it destroys any reasonable perspective on those careers. It is in this life that we are to achieve happiness and do good. Of no other life have we usable knowledge.

Arguments have been offered based on reports by those who have "come back from death (so-called) to life" remembering remarkable experiences of how it was after their hearts stopped beating and their lungs stopped inhaling and they were in that sense dead. But the fact that these persons did retain or regain consciousness is sufficient evidence for the uninterrupted aliveness of their brain cells, upon which, and not directly upon heart or lungs, consciousness depends. This tells us nothing at all about what it will be like when our brain cells are dead.

Religion and Philosophy

Not only do religious people need to open their minds to science, in its basic spiritual vision or attitude, but they also need to have some appreciation for the role of philosophy, with all the latter's manifest limitations and inability to reach anything like a stable consensus. For as science is the cooperative, public-spirited, intellectual search for the hidden beauties of nature, which believers in God must take as manifestations of the divine, or as the really superhuman "word of God," so philosophy is the cooperative (though facing greater difficulties of communication), public-spirited, intellectual search for principles so fundamental that they can mediate between science and religion, or between one religion and another. It can help us to decide what to do about the stubborn fact attested to by all history that in civilized societies consensus in religion, otherwise than by brute force (and then only through hypocrisy and the stifling of individual curiosity or inquiry) is not a practical goal, at least for any future that we can foresee. I regard the lack of philosophical literacy in some circles in this country as a danger to our democracy. The one-issue fanatics in politics are insufficiently disciplined philosophically, and they are a danger to the democratic process as such.

In a televised discussion of "creation biology" versus evolution, a Louisiana man explained candidly his need to accept creation biology by the statements that he needed an anchor in life, that he found it in the Bible, but that, if God "lies to him" in part of the Bible, he cannot trust God to be telling the truth in other parts. The following implications of this defence are remarkable.

It is implied that reading the Bible is fully equivalent to having a conversation with God, or at least to reading letters in the divine handwriting. It is implied that this man has no knowledge of life, of nature, of the varied thoughts of great minds about life and nature, no experience of good and evil, sufficient to give him norms by which to discriminate degrees of truth or levels of meaning in the Bible. It is also implied that every mistake in the Bible must mean that someone is lying, or indeed that God is lying. Yet this very man, thus innocent of any sense that he can rely upon of value or importance, or of how to interpret documents written in a very different culture from ours (devoid of our science and technology, our philosophy, and much else), claims to be able to know or to reasonably believe that one book is *the* book, all of which must be absolutely true, or else of no religious help at all. There are many books for which similar claims are made. For Islam it is the *Koran,* for Hindus the *Bhagavad Gita,* for multitudes of Chinese the *I Ching* or the *Analects* of Confucius, for Christian Scientists the book by Mary Baker Eddy. For Jews the Old Testament is the entire Bible. Our Louisiana citizen is disagreeing with all of these and countless others as well, including millions of nonfundamentalist Christians. How, without criteria which would enable him to see more truth in some parts of the Bible than in others, can he possibly form a reasonable judgment as to whether the Bible, or even whether any possible human book, could be the infallible God addressing us in human words in such fashion that we could not be mistaken as to the meaning, or as to the lesson we could wisely draw from the words?

I have some fear of that Louisiana man (for whom I also feel compassion) and others like him. For they would be willing to have certain aspects of their view enacted into law, backed by the powers of the police. The only justification I can see for this attitude is that our all-too-government-controlled educational system has already used that same police power to tax people to pay for education in public schools, whether or not parents or pupils like what is taught in those schools. This is a rather baffling political dilemma we have drifted into, thanks to our insufficient belief in freedom. If we had more freedom than we have in education I would see no excuse whatever for the government's doing anything to help along such an intellectually unimpressive cause as that of trying to derive knowledge of nature from a book written by those who had incomparably less of that knowledge than we have. But the dilemma spoken of is real.

Compare the text that Eve was made from Adam's rib with the texts that announce the two commandments of how and what to love as summing up the essence of religion. Everything some of us feel we have learned from life and literature seems to support the commandments, nothing of it supports one of the two Genesis accounts of the origin of the female half of the species. The other account simply says, "Male and female created he them." True, we are not God, not infallible. But then how could anyone, not infallible, have much confidence in his or her ability to know that a certain book must be either infallible (something it is close to meaningless to say of a book) or else have *no* wisdom to give us? An educational system that does not enable people to think in a more informed and disciplined way than that Louisiana man evidences is perhaps not good enough to be supported by general taxation.

Our Constitution rightly separates church and state. But can education and religion be equally separated? We need more consideration of that side of the question. I am not happy with the currently available answers. And I write as an emeritus professor of a state university. However, I am grateful that my own higher education was all private.

Since there is no clear consensus either in philosophy or in religion, it behooves teachers (writers, lawmakers) to be careful about presuming to narrow the options that individuals face in choosing basic beliefs. To try to bully readers or hearers into a choice between just the two possibilities, a Godless belief in evolution, or a belief in God that excludes evolution, is to mistreat people. There is no support in philosophy for the exclusion of a third option, belief in God that includes belief in evolution. And there is no consensus in theology for this exclusion either. To suppose otherwise is to be unaware of the actual state of knowledge in our time.

A religion and philosophy of freedom must try to teach people to keep asking the question,"Does this or that procedure unduly narrow the options for individual choice?" "Creation biology or else a Godless biology" is a cruel, as well as an ignorant, dilemma. Nor is there any consensus for the view that a fetus has all the value of a person, and that its destruction is thus murder in the same sense as any other homicide. Even if a bare majority in Congress or state legislatures could be attained, it would be tyranny to impose this view by the police power. There are many of us who deeply believe this. The fetus is "human" biologically; but the issue is one of ethics and law, not of mere biology: it transcends natural science.

Pollsters are telling us that a substantial majority of the citizens of this country believe in God. As a believer, I find this encouraging. In Europe it seems that believers are perhaps a minority. But, alas, I strongly suspect that in Europe literal-minded fundamentalists are a much smaller proportion of believers than is the case here. As a non-literal-minded believer I find this fact discouraging, almost frightening. Given enough political power to fundamentalists, how close might we come to a new Inquisition, that great monstrosity which disfigured traditional Christianity? Religious fanaticism is still with us, and it has had an ugly history.

A friend, a theologian, had a phrase that has stuck with me, "the acidity of orthodoxy." Orthodoxy can be worse than acid. It can be lethal. I have encountered a "pro-lifer" who gave me little sense of being pro my life or the life of adults generally. Pro-fetus-life is a very special form of enthusiasm for life. I have respect for the fetus as, like all animals, a wondrous creation, and a suitable object of sympathy. In addition it is capable of eventually, with much help from relatively adult persons, of becoming first an infant (and then a child), beginning to learn from its elders, and finally an adult human person. We are all human *individuals* long before we are *persons* in the value sense of actually thinking and reasoning in the human fashion. Even in dreamless sleep as adults, we are not actually functioning as persons; but this does not abolish the obviously crucial difference between a fetus whose potentiality for rational personhood requires at least many months of help by actual persons to be actualized even slightly, and a sleeping adult who has already functioned as a person for many years and who has made many plans for what it will do in its waking moments, perhaps for years to come.

The spell of tradition, taking over part of the function of instinct, is the wall that staves off chaos in human behavior. It may be that many simply must go on believing in survival in the rather naive form, as it seems to the rest of us, that we are all familiar with. But it cannot be right to try to prevent individuals who feel no need for this belief from nevertheless believing in God as the only immortal being—save as the objective immortality of the past in God makes us and all creatures permanent divine possessions. Accepting the two commandments said to sum up Biblical religion is one thing, belief in tall tales about human careers after death is another and, in my judgment, incomparably less important one. It is hard enough, though I find it personally not too hard, to believe firmly in God, without having also to believe in those tales. The arguments for theistic belief that I have carefully formulated (with so far scarcely a word of rebuttal) in my book *Creative Synthesis and Philosophic Method* do not support infinite careers for human animals. That is a radically different belief from any reasonable point of view. It requires us to add to our observational knowledge of our species and its place among the animals on this planet an *infinite* addition making our species not only radically more intelligent than the others but, in one respect, as different in status from the others as God is believed to be to creatures generally. This not only does not follow from belief in God but tends to make God a mere means to our everlasting happiness and to make each of us a rival to God in endurance and ability to preserve personal individuality through an infinity of experiences without monotony or loss of integrity.

The central question of religion cannot be, "What about heaven and hell?" but must be, "What about God, cosmic mind and love, exalted in principle above all else, the only indestructible, all-inclusive, yet individual, being?"

The belief that God does not simply and completely make things, but brings it about that they partly make themselves and one another, does not mean that the divine creating is just one more case of creating. In principle, the divine action has unrivaled superiority. Most obviously it is divine decision which determines the form of the statistical or approximate cosmic orderliness, leaving the details for the creatures to settle. What physicists are trying to discover are, as some of them have said, divine thoughts by which the creatures are, not (we are learning to say) *determined*, but so *influenced* that abstract regularities or laws apply to the results. Finally, it is divine decision which determines *how* creaturely experiences are to be objectively *immortalized* and so achieve the only importance they will ultimately have. Thus, to quote from a Jewish ritual, God "gives to our fleeting days abiding significance." Our value to posterity extends this significance, but without God it would ultimately fade away toward nothingness, so far as human wit has been able to grasp this problem. The species cannot be known to forever escape destruction from cosmic forces and its own folly, and posterity's ability to use our lives for its own welfare or enjoyment is unpredictable and certainly limited. Only God can be guaranteed to make ideally wise use of what we have been.

Several objections to the foregoing are foreseeable. One is that if all God is doing is giving the world an orderliness by which creaturely freedom (and hence chance) have their limited place and to immortalize creaturely experiences in and for His-Her own life, this is too little to do for the creatures. Also, it makes God ultimately selfish. Finally, it is God who receives all rewards, not any creatures. These objections imply a somewhat complex defence, if defence is possible.

First, I wish to insist that it is no small thing to give the world sufficient orderliness to make it possible for free creatures (that is, creatures) to adapt to one another essentially harmoniously. Every organism is an internal harmony, proportional to its health, while it lives, and healthy organisms are bound to predominate in nature. The cosmic harmony is an infinite good, at least in the sense that without it there would be no good worth mentioning, and that, if the creative advance is beginningless and endless (as I hold), there is no upper limit to the value produced. It is not to be supposed a simple, slight thing that a being, by its own influence, orders all other things so that the opportunities for good expressions of freedom justify the risks of more-or-less evil or unfortunate expressions. How such ordering is possible exceeds our human imagination to grasp. It is a mystery in the best sense of that word. And belief in it gives meaning to our lives.

Second, I know of no proof that God's influence upon the creatures is only that expressed by the natural laws giving order to worldly happenings. From the unsurpassable power and wisdom of God I deduce that *if* the divine influence would produce better results for the beauty of the world by going beyond the mere ordering in question, then the influence does go farther. But I doubt our human wisdom to know if this further limiting of freedom would produce better results. All I do think I know is that the opportunities involved in a given degree of freedom tend to increase only with a corresponding increase in risks. Primitive man had more freedom, more opportunity, with more risks of doing harm than other animals; we, with our science and technology, have still more scope for our decision-making, and we can do much more harm and much more good. This is what I see clearly. Whether, or how far, miracles happen, as recorded in every religion, I do not know and see no way to decide. I cannot live and die for their having occurred or their having not occurred. The meaning of life for me is independent of that question.

Is God Selfish?

The charge that a being is selfish unless it can do good to others without this good being of use to itself is a curious confusion, almost comical when looked at calmly and analytically. Save me from a friend who says to me, "The good that results to you from my being and acting is nothing in my life. I am totally unmoved and ungratified by the benefits my action brings to you. Whether you live or die, enjoy or suffer, is all one to me. My own possession of good is in every respect totally independent of any good in you. I am like the sun, bestowing benefits without the results giving me anything I would otherwise lack. I am absolutely unselfish, that is, I do not rejoice in your joy, or sorrow in your sorrow."

The situation, looked at carefully, seems as follows. It is human beings who do not, and could not possibly, get the full value of the good they bring to others. By the time a good deed reaches its result in the other, the benefactor may be dead or far away and know nothing about it. At best, no human being can fully share in the experiences he or she helps others to enjoy. Nor can we fully share in the sufferings we cause others. Our limited power to perceive and understand guarantees that. Hence there is need for us to be willing to furnish others with values we are ourselves unable to fully profit from. Every parent or teacher experiences this. Accordingly, we will, if we are ethical, try to bring good to others some of which can never become our good. But quite obviously all of this arises from our limitations, none of which is applicable to God. God cannot possibly miss the enjoyment of any beauty divinely given to others. The final harvest from every seed sown is reaped by God. And this is the meaning of divine cognitive-perceptive perfection. In that sense Deity is indeed absolute perfection. So the traditional version of the divine unselfishness is the attribution to God of an absolute form of the relative defects which distinguish the creatures from God!

God is neither selfish nor unselfish as we exhibit these traits. Rather, God is unsurpassably loving, and that means fully grasping the good of others as *therefore also* divine good. God's satisfaction includes all the satisfactions of others, integrated on a higher level into the satisfaction which surpasses that of any conceivable other but perpetually exceeds itself as new others arise to enrich it.

Note, too, that if God participates more fully in our happiness than we can in that of one another, it also follows that God participates more fully in our suffering. Vicarious suffering is the only meaning of divine unselfishness, and process theology (Berdyaev, Whitehead) fully accepts this. The cross is Christianity's sublime symbol. Would that, in its doctrine of the divine perfection, it had made more use of what is thus symbolized!

A further objection to the concept of creaturely good as finally contributory to divine good (and only therewith immortal) is that it does not give us a sufficient rational aim to say that we can contribute to a divine good when our lives are over. We shall not be there, still conscious of God's enjoyment of our having lived. Here, too, I see confusion. Our consciousness, *so far as there ever has been such a thing as our consciousness,* will still be there in God. It will be such consciousness as we had before dying, but all of it will be imperishable in God. If we are now aware of ourselves as contributing to the divine consciousness, that very awareness of God's awareness of us will not perish but "live forevermore" (Whitehead). What will not be there are new, additional states of awareness belonging to us, other than those we had before dying.

Divine Love as the Meaning of Life

If I am told that it is asking too much freedom from egocentricity to expect human beings to accept the imperishable divine enjoyment of our earthly lives as a sufficient aim for human endeavor, I can only reply, "What then did you have in mind when you accepted, if you did, the great commandment to love God with *all* your being? Did you then hold back with the proviso, 'Assuming that God *forever* keeps on giving *me* new joys and blessings—otherwise I refuse to play'?" Just as people have not taken seriously the second commandment, to love the neighbor as the self, so they have not taken really seriously the first commandment. My proposal is that we accept both as meaning what they say and *as among the most exact expressions of an idea to be found outside of pure and applied mathematics.*

God is not to be bargained with. We are contingent beings. We might not have existed, and so long as we live it is our will to live that keeps us alive. "The universe," as Stephen Crane implied in a poem, is not in debt to us. The reward for living is the living itself. Anything more is a bonus. It is other creatures who may owe us things, and with whom we may bargain. There was a man

who said, "I am willing to be damned for the glory of God."
Would this excellent fellow have been willing, for the divine glory,
to admit that there might be no such things as damnation or as
being assigned to purgatory or heaven? The glory of God is everything or nothing. It is the absolute measure of value.

What then does God do for us? Divine action makes our existence
possible, with all its moments of joy and tolerable sorrow (the
intolerable deprives us of consciousness), and in addition gives us
a rational aim and possibility of making wise, caring decisions in
such fashion that, in the long run and on the whole, those we
love, including ourselves and our human posterity, will probably
(because the world is ordered) have better lives than if we decide
carelessly or selfishly. Also, and in any case, whatever good qualities
of experience we enjoy, or help others to enjoy, will be indestructible elements in the Life, love for which is, so far as we understand
ourselves, our inclusive concern. If there is any serious rival to this
as an aim I do not know of it.

The wise and almost unbelievedly neglected Fechner said it over
a century ago: "To find one's satisfaction in satisfying God, as that
one who finds greatest satisfaction in the utmost possible satisfaction
of all—higher than this no feeling of satisfaction can go."[2]

I do not recall Fechner referring to Plato, but I think Plato
would have been keenly interested in the following:

> However high any being (other than God) stands, it still has
> an external world; other beings, similar to it, limit it; only as
> it rises higher does it contain more within itself, exist more
> purely within itself.
> But God, as the totality of being . . . has no external en-
> vironment, no beings outside himself; . . . is one and unique;
> all spirits move in the inner world of his spirit; all bodies in
> the inner world of his body.[3]

These passages from Fechner show that Plato's vision of the
World Soul, God as the cosmic, ideal animal, was not lost forever.
Spinoza, following the Stoics, had a version of it; but Spinoza's
version was ruined by determinism, the denial of freedom in either
God or creatures. Spinoza talked of creation, but he emptied the

concept of meaning by likening it to the way a triangle has three angles. Recently Strawson, widely influential British philosopher, has suggested that what philosophy can regard as worthy of the veneration formerly directed to God is "the universe." If that means simply "the inclusive reality," well and good. But much depends upon how one conceives the inclusive reality. A few among modern theologians (the saintly D. C. McIntosh, for one) have used the mind-body analogy. There is really no substitute for it. But any basic misconception of the human or higher-animal basis of the analogy will cause trouble in the theological use of it. To this extent there was some ground for the medieval suspicion of it.

Some will say that identifying God with the inclusive reality is "pantheism." Once more, it depends on how "the inclusive reality" is conceived. Conceived deterministically, with no freedom allowed to the included constituents or members, the analogy ruins theology. But it also prevents any real understanding of the ordinary animal case. Allow some freedom to the bodily members (cells or other micro-elements) and the theory begins to work. Allow, further, at least minimal sentience to the members, so that the relationship can be one of sympathy, feeling of others' feelings, and it works better still. Allow, as freedom implies, that the members create something of themselves, one another, and the soul of the whole, and vice versa, and it works best of all. So much for the ambiguous charge of "pantheism."

Some readers will be worried about the question, "Is not the injunction 'Love the other as oneself' utterly beyond human capacity to obey?" I answer, "It is the absolute ideal, and therefore not a literal description of how people behave." Only divine decisions literally express an absolute idea. This is why it is unbecoming to boast of one's unselfishness or charity. We can all see in others the rationalizations of selfishness of which human ingenuity is capable. But the ideal, however transcendent of our capacities, is relevant as showing us exactly what it would be like to be ethically infallible. It is also relevant as showing us what it would be like to be completely rational about conflicting interests. It is not rational to value oneself for various personal qualities rated by norms of value which, applied accurately and fairly, would show the other equally or more valuable, and yet put a higher value on oneself simply because one is oneself and the other is the other. Self-love is natural enough, but it is not reason or the principle of rationality.

By animal feeling one is the center of the universe: I here, everyone else there. Reason tells another story. The other is as much the center as the self. This contrast is the human condition. Egocentricity is an illusion pervading our lives, but we *know* that it is an illusion. The idea of God is the idea of a being that really is the seat of all value. Nothing is valuable unless valuable to God. As Niebuhr was so brilliant in pointing out, we are tempted to put ourselves in the place we know belongs properly only to God.

The value equality of self as such and other as such does not mean that we do not for practical reasons have special responsibilities for our own welfare. There are many benefits which no one can give to us unless we give them to ourselves. Kant was very right in talking about a *duty* to make oneself happy. Those who neglect their own health or other conditions of happiness will end up being a nuisance or worse for others. Who wants an unhappy spouse, unhappy neighbor or friend, least of all if the unhappiness is largely the individual's own fault? There is also the need to bear in mind the difficulty of knowing what really will benefit another whose tastes or wishes we may not understand. That "do-gooders" are sometimes nuisances or tyrants is only too true. But there are, nevertheless, times and circumstances when altruistic behavior is a blessing and inspiration to those it intends to help and to others who behold it. Sometimes it saves a drowning person at real risk. Sometimes it transforms the character of a previously lost soul, as in Victor Hugo's story about the thief and the bishop.

Charles Peirce, considering what the ideal of good behavior is like, suggested that a mother of several children, with a good attitude toward those children, is a fair model to think about. I had such a mother and I agree with him. I argued often with my mother and even grieved her sometimes by this. But I recall no instance when I thought her selfish toward any of us. I know of *no one* needlessly offended by her, no instance of even the slightest tinge of cruelty. Yet she had no morbid idea that her own happiness was to be neglected. After, as an old lady, she was widowed and had inherited most of her husband's money, at her own initiative, in consultation with a financially shrewd son, she divided some of the money among the rest of us. She would always pay our fare to travel to her place of retirement. As she put it, with a smile, "My money is for my own pleasure and it is my pleasure to have you visit me . . ." But if for a good long time we did not come there were no complaints. She really did approximate living by the second as well as the first great commandment. Even in marked senility, no sign of greed or resentment appeared. Her kindness went all through. True, she did, in imagination kill off a younger sister who was very much alive a thousand miles away—"I'm the only one left [of the seven Haughton children]." But this only showed that she was human, after all. She also confessed, "I never liked my mother," something she would not have said when in better health. But her mother was less kind and gentle than she was—also less humorous—and the incompatibility between the two was intelligible and hardly her fault.

The memory of my mother is one of many which make it impossible for me to respond positively to the suggestion heard so often that, apart from the account of the life of Jesus, or even, apart from the Bible as a whole, we would know nothing about God. "Speak for yourself," is what I feel I must say to this. The Hymns of Ikhnaton, naive in some ways as they are, would almost convince me, and in some respects they make points I miss in the Bible (the idea of self-creation is there, for instance, as it is in a pre-Columbian Mexican poet of long ago, "The creator of all is self-created.") The idea of a God of love has dawned on many in many lands and at many times. There is no book the absence of which would leave us helpless to arrive at this idea. It was found in China, India, pre-Christian Palestine; an approach to it was known by the Amerindians, some of them at least. Plato almost had it: in certain respects he came closer to it than the medieval theologians.

On the other hand, I am in no position to say what would have happened to my religious development had my parents and several teachers at school not been Christians well trained in relatively orthodox ways. And the parables of Jesus seem to me full of wisdom; incidents like the washing of the disciples' feet, or the forgiveness from the cross, seem full of symbolic power to convey religious insight.

On a less positive note, I believe—with Peirce, Whitehead, D. H. Lawrence (three rather different persons) and my father (different still)—that the Book of Revelation is a poor expression of a religion of love, for the very reasons these four agreed upon: that it expresses hate, arrogance, resentment, and superstition run riot. It ought, as they held, to have been omitted from the Canon. So there we have it—consensus in religion is out of our reach. We have to agree to disagree.

Consensus in politics is also difficult to attain, but without a minimum of it our species is doomed. The development of nuclear explosives, perhaps even the possession of poisons (in present stocks, it is said, capable of poisoning the entire population of the world), has brought us to this degree of danger. Thus the perilous "experiment of nature," a species as free from instinctive guidance as ours, is approaching its critical stage. Was the experiment too dangerous? As theist I accept on faith the infallible wisdom and ideal power of God. But if I play at criticizing God it is at this point.

Why There Is Human Wickedness

To the question, "Why is there so much wickedness in human beings?" our culture knows two answers. One is the biblical Garden of Eden story, interpreted as an account of how sinfulness became innate in us all, the theory of Original Sin. The other is the scientific and evolutionary account, including psychiatry as a part of science—though not necessarily the psychoanalysis of Freud and Jung. The Garden of Eden account has all the marks of a very tall tale, with its highly unnatural serpent and much else. Moreover, there is no evidence whatever that its author or authors had the slightest knowledge of the possibility of an evolutionary account of the origin of species, including ours. It is an axiom of intellectual procedure that to have a fully rational right to adopt a philosophical or scientific belief one must have considered what other explanations (taken in their strongest not their weakest form) could be offered to solve the same problem. Biblical authors did not reject evolution. There is no sign that they knew of it as a possible theory.

In their ignorance they did what they could to understand human nature. Today we have not their excuse for the result.

According to evolution, animals are enabled to serve the needs of their species and to take their place in nature without needless damage to other species (definitely including those whose members they prey on) by two factors: *instinct,* or physically inherited modes of behavior, and *culture,* or psychically inherited modes of behavior. In the lower animals the instinctive or physical inheritance predominates, in the higher animals the cultural or psychical more and more takes over as one ascends the hierarchy toward the human species. On all levels there is an aspect of freedom with its chance combinations of decisions. This aspect implies that neither laws of nature nor the decision of any agent can make all of these combinations fortunate ones, exactly conforming to some ideal plan or arrangement for the good of the whole. What fits the needs of one organism may not fit the needs of another. Conflict and suffering cannot be wholly excluded; there will be good luck as well as bad luck for particular individuals. On the lower levels such conflicts involve no wickedness, for the creatures are essentially instinctive; their individual decisions, though not wholly determined by either instinct or culture, are too naive, too little conscious, to involve any comparison of their action with an ethical principle of right and wrong. On higher levels, perhaps only on the highest (the human), there is such comparison. Now *either/or:* the individuals on this high level are ethically infallible (capable of acting rightly, knowing that they are doing so, but incapable of acting wrongly, knowing that they are doing so) *or* all animals capable of being ethical are capable of lapsing from their ethical norms. Not only is it the fact that human beings are fallible ethically, but it seems infinitely unlikely that they should be othewise. Infallibility is a property of deity. Only God is either cognitively infallible or incapable of unwise or unrighteous behavior. Does not ethical or practical infallibility belong with cognitive infallibility? Unsurpassable power, unsurpassable wisdom, unsurpassable goodness—these define God, not any mere creature.

In the foregoing I have transcended the merely biological and introduced theological considerations. Let us return to the biological problem. Chance, or good and bad luck, occurs on all levels of life, for reasons already explained. This implies suffering and frustration in varying degrees. At their births, and often thereafter, human beings suffer. With good luck the sufferings of birth are slight, with bad luck, severe. There are evolutionary reasons why totally painless birth is unlikely, perhaps impossible. There are similar evolutionary reasons why there will be infectious diseases, which are the good luck of bacteria or virus organisms causing the bad luck of the host organism. To wholly prevent these things would impose further limitations on the freedom of creatures to *make themselves* (and in part their descendants, thus causing evolutionary change). What sort of world, far from ours in structure, if even a coherent world at all, this further limitation on freedom would imply takes perhaps more insight into world possibilities than we possess.

We are, then, a species of animal whose members must at times suffer. This is true of all species, but the members of our species are peculiarly sensitive and capable of suffering in a far greater variety of ways than other sorts of animals, with complex mental as well as merely physical forms of suffering or frustration. Moreover, in this species (for good reasons) the young are born radically helpless and immature, devoid of the sense of right and wrong they will later acquire. If their parents or caretakers are themselves suffering severe frustrations, their nervous systems irritated to the breaking point, or if they have escaped the cultural inheritance without which the human deficiency of physical inheritance, or lack of instinctive wisdom, means incompetent treatment of offspring, then the offspring are likely to be badly treated. Remember, the parents are mere creatures and hence fallible. How then will the offspring react to the bad treatment they receive? Because of their immaturity, their pre-ethical stage, they cannot react in an ethically noble way, with forgiveness and compassion for the parents' deficiency or the parents' suffering. To bad treatment they can only react more or less badly, either by violent rebellion and active hatred, or—probably even worse—by sullen apathy, passive hatred. Thus their emotional development begins badly.

One can often, alas, on public vehicles, such as trains or planes, see parents obviously engaged in ruining their offspring (by treating them with hatred and cruelty). It is not only Freud who has taught us how important these early misfortunes are in the formation of human characters. Harry Stack Sullivan, whom I have read, and another American psychiatrist, whom I have heard lecture, have been my teachers in this matter. I think they give a far better explanation, not indeed of original sin, but of what tends to produce wicked behavior, than any tall story written long ago.

There is, however, a theological aspect which can be taken to complete the merely biological account. As Reinhold Niebuhr, in his inimitable way, has pointed out, our unique human capacity to form general ideas, including the extremely general idea of the Creator of all, opens us to a form of temptation unique to our species. So far as we know what it would be like to be God, we also know what we lack by not being God. The other animals, we may surmise, share with us the status of creaturehood but, unlike us, do not at all know what it would be like to be the universal Creator. But—and here the plot thickens—Niebuhr sees that we can to some extent deceive ourselves and imagine that we are not quite mere creatures, that somehow we are ourselves infallible, all-wise, or all-powerful: if not without qualification, then still sufficiently so for whatever it is we have set our hearts upon. We can try to play at being more than in truth we possibly can be.

"Playing God" is a phrase that can be sadly misused. Example: if a surgeon operates, some religious groups complain that he is not accepting an individual as God made that individual. If a doctor helps a patient with a terminal disease to die, he is said to be taking God's role. This charge makes sense only on the assumption that it is God who normally completely determines what happens to us (for example when we die), not our own decisions or those of other creatures.

Those so talking do not, by my standards, know what they are talking about. They are less well informed than they think they are as to what the role of God really is. If they are not playing God, they are certainly to a questionable extent playing at being "in the know" about God. At any rate, Niebuhr may well be right in his view that one form of wickedness arises from not fully accepting our creaturehood, our not being God. Politically powerful individuals are exposed to this temptation. But so is a father in an old-fashioned male-dominated family.

I submit that a theologically interpreted evolutionism can do a better job than anything written over two thousand years ago to explain human wickedness. It can even adopt one element of the Eden story: what made Adam's "fall" possible was his "knowledge of good and evil." This is inherent in his ability to conceive deity. It also is inherent in his symbolic power, his ability for speech, including maps, diagrams, graphs, musical notations, sign posts, and representative drawings and paintings. Other animals on this planet (there may be billions of planets) lack these capacities in any remotely comparable degree. But with this symbolic power goes a partial freedom from physical inheritance of behavior, and with this a danger of social chaos and failure to serve the needs of the species or to take our place in nature without needless damage to other species, all of which functions instincts admirably serve.

When wolves or coyotes kill many sheep at a time, far more than they can eat, this is not because their natures or instincts are wrong as such, but because instinct cannot adapt to conditions which until quite recently did not obtain in the part of the earth where the instinct developed. Herds of sheep, weakened and made helpless by domestication for many generations, are a novelty for North American animals. In their natural environment, wolves do not decimate quantities of sheep or any other kind of animal. The wild sheep of the Rockies did quite well, thank you, for thousands of years, until civilized human beings came along. Among animals it is only the human species that makes ugly gaps and desolations in nature. Albert Schweitzer (who respected animal life but, as a biologist friend has pointed out, failed to understand it) was morally indignant at a leopard that slaughtered the chickens in the coop he had constructed so badly that, though the leopard could get in, the chickens could not get out. It would be a fortunate leopard that could catch even two chickens or other large birds in the open forest as easily as that leopard caught many almost at once. Incidentally, it was like a human being to blame the leopard, or nature, for what was primarily his own doing.

If we cannot hope to see wickedness as God sees it, we can nevertheless have some partial grasp of the truth that, being a creature (in the fashion in which each of us is that, localized in space-time, having to acquire personality, beginning with merely animal individuality, taught how to behave as a person by fallible elders, themselves taught by fallible elders, and so on), we cannot have the infallible rightness of behavior that is a defining characteristic of deity.

I add a thought that, so far as I know, I am the first philosopher to say clearly and definitely: To describe our difference from God as infinite by calling us "finite" is far too little. We are much *less* than simply finite. The entire vast cosmos may be (and I believe is) spatially finite, as relativity physics has made clear it may be. We, however, are the merest fragments of finite reality. *Fragmentariness, not simply finitude, distinguishes us from deity.* With this fragmentariness goes radical dependence upon our surroundings, by which we can be destroyed at any time. True, "destruction" here does not mean that our careers up to the moment of death are nullified, made into nothing, for that is nonsense. But our careers can have in each case a last member, as a book a last word; whereas the real divine book reaches no last word, just as it has had no first one, and is in that respect infinite. And in that infinite book our finite ones are imperishable.

Is God in every sense infinite? According to dual transcendence this cannot be. God has a spatial aspect; the divine "ubiquity" is God's presence everywhere in space; but if space is finite, then so is the divine ubiquity. Moreover, if the spatial expansion of the cosmos is possible, God's spatial finitude can also expand. But what canot be is that God should be a mere fragment of the spatial whole, as each of us is.

Nuclear Arms

In the present situation the greatest practical threat of all is possibility of nuclear war. Since there is no way now known (if you question this, do a little research in the subject) that promises to prevent nuclear war from being nuclear annihilation of at least most of our population, and much else besides around the world, the aim of nuclear arms is not to enable us to win in nuclear war but to enable us to prevent there being any such war. As the

Russian Khrushchev said years ago, if country A can and in a nuclear war would destroy country B twice over, and country B can (and would) destroy A once over, neither country has a rational reason to use nuclear arms. So all talk about parity in numbers of nuclear weapons is absurd. We could reduce the world largely to rubble and death. So could the Russians.

Is it sensible to ask the Russians to give up what we (wrongly) tell the world is an advantage in nuclear armaments? If they are so unwise as to believe what we thus unwisely tell them, then of course they will not agree to reduce armaments to come down to parity with us. Mutual ability to destroy is the only relevant parity in the matter, if the aim is deterrence.

It seems foolish diplomacy to expect to accomplish anything by threatening to catch up to the Russians in excessive armaments unless they agree to reduce numbers down to ours. If superiority in numbers really is an advantage, and they have that advantage (as some of us assert), what can we offer the Russians to give it up? We should tell them we think it no advantage, and we should prove that we mean what we say by unilateral reduction, not down to less than is needed for deterrence—meaning ability to destroy the enemy were he so mad as to provoke us—but with the sole purpose of giving him no motive for doing so.

We should stop letting what Russia is doing militarily dictate our military budget and further ruin our economy with the inflation that goes with such a policy. We should free our policy from slavish dependence on what Russia is doing in armaments, and encourage the Russians to follow our example as we try to attend to the economic needs of our people, also to free our society, as Eisenhower warned us we should do, from excessive dependence on the industrial-military complex, which today threatens our economy and makes the Reagan policy partly self-contradictory. Militarism is anti-economical. Japan and Germany show what a blessing it can be if a country controls its military caste or military-industrial complex. Our best hope may be that Russia will begin to see the point and will do more for its nonmilitary industries and agriculture than its present militarism allows it to do.

Whether or not Theodore Draper is right in regarding a "no first use" of nuclear arms declaration as of questionable value, the overwhelmingly important point, for which Draper argues so persuasively, is that they should not be used at all.[4] If we had been more civilized than we are, we might have done better not to have used them twice ourselves. We set an ominous example.

A nuclear freeze would be better than nothing. But the only significant aim is reduction. We should try to lead the world in this, without looking over our shoulder too anxiously to see what others are doing. We should show that we know our own minds and have our own convictions, above all the conviction that explosives with virtually unlimited destructive powers have no sane use except to prevent others from using them. There is only one planet, and if we incinerate and poison much of it, all our hopes are doomed, not just our hopes of victory. The Russians must, it seems, know all this; we should show enough respect for them as not complete fools to act as if we knew that they know it. If they don't know it, negotiations will not help. If they do, negotiations should be about matters other than who has the most nuclear weapons.

The foregoing is, of course, an amateur's view; but I have read a good many discussions by experts, including many issues of the *Bulletin of Atomic Scientists,* and listened to a number of speeches by authorities on the medical aspects of nuclear warfare, than which a more dismal, horrible topic of contemplation can scarcely be imagined. In comparison, talk of a supernatural hell seems childish folly.

God and the Universe Once More

For Plato, the universe was the divine body, for Goethe it was the "living garment of deity." If the divine body, or garment, is spatially finite, this does not do away with its radical superiority to our bodies or garments. There is nothing outside it by which it could be injured or disturbed. As for what is inside it, this cannot threaten it either, as cancer cells threaten us. For the divine-human analogy assumes a difference in principle between the ideal animal and all others, or between the nonfragmentary organism and the fragmentary organisms. The human infant begins to impose a secondary life-style expressive of its feelings (and thoughts, as fast as it becomes able to think) upon a system which already had a basic order in its cells and their inherited and acquired patterns, all of this expressive of the general laws of nature. But these laws themselves express the World Soul and its unsurpassable mode of awareness and feeling. The World Soul does not begin to exist on a foundation otherwise established.

When an animal dies and its individual life-style no longer controls its members, the result is not chaos, but simply a return to the more pervasive types of order expressive of the cosmic mind-body. The World Soul, being aware of what occurs in the Divine Body, can vicariously suffer with its suffering members (Plato did not say so, but we can say it). But it cannot suffer in the sense of having fear of an alien force. This Soul's power is the unrivaled, eminent power. Any individual can influence it, none can threaten it. Its life-style is the supreme law of the whole.

There must, it seems, be readers who have been thinking: a World Soul implies a world brain, and there is no such thing. I have in principle given—indeed, Plato gave—the answer to this objection. A central nervous system, with its brain, is, as already remarked, the quintessential body of an ordinary or human vertebrate animal. But the contrast between that and less essential bodily parts arises from the animal's having an external environment. Our awareness is most directly conditioned by our nerve cells. The rest is but means to the functioning of those cells, so far as the possibility of our awareness is concerned. Plato began his analysis by pointing out that the cosmos needs no limbs to enable it to move about, for it is its own place (space being merely the order among its parts); it needs no digestive system to transform materials taken in from without into bodily tissue and no lungs to enable it to utilize air from without; for nothing is without. So with all organs outside the central nervous system. Plato did not understand that system; but we can see that is is not only the seat of consciousness, but is also the means of adapting internal activities to external stimuli. This function cannot apply to the inclusive organism.

Thinking out the question of the role of a body for its soul, we realize that, with no external environment, the sole function of the supreme Body for the supreme Soul is to furnish it with awareness of and power over its bodily members. Thus there can be no special parts, such as brain cells, in contrast to other parts; for all have the same function of directly communicating with the Soul. Thus every physical individual in the Body becomes as a nerve or brain cell to the Soul. There can therefore be no *special* part of the cosmos recognizable as a nervous system. The whole cosmos must everywhere directly communicate with God, each member furnishing its own psychical content (its feelings or thoughts) to the Soul. In turn, the member, in whatever way its own type of individuality makes possible, and across the two-way bridge of sympathy or feeling of feeling, receives influences from divine feeling or thought.

Such is my attempt to indicate and profit by the way various thinkers—Fechner, Whitehead, and some others—have tried to go further along the path first blazed by Plato.

The great theoretical physicist Hermann Weyl once wrote, "If the space-time whole is not divine it is certainly superhuman." I think he understated the case.

In the foregoing discussion, I have not mentioned the Big Bang account of current physics. I am little competent to discuss it. But I do hold the considered conviction that it is not a proper role for physics to attempt to deal with really ultimate questions. I doubt, on principle, the possibility of knowledge by empirical, observational science to the effect that, for instance, the Big Bang and its consequences constitute the whole of created reality, before which there was not anything (or only God); or that there could never have been and could never be other laws of nature than those now obtaining. We cannot, with any cogency, extrapolate our stretch of observed cosmic happenings to infinity, nor can we know that a Big Bang beyond which we cannot extrapolate can have had no predecessor. With Berdyaev, I believe in a divine time, our access to which is not unlimited, to say the least. Time as we know it best may indeed have begun with the Big Bang, but not all time, creaturely or divine. The integration of physics into a comprehensive system inclusive of philosophical principles is an achievement for the future. I envy those who, if the species endures in spite of its present hazards, will some day manage to work out and understand such a system. What a splendid achievement that will be!

Notes

1. Harry Kemelman, *Thursday the Rabbi Walked Out* (New York: Fawcett Crest, 1978), pp. 229–30.
2. See Hartshorne and Reese, *Philosophers Speak of God* (University of Chicago Press, 1953), p. 251, 1st column.
3. Ibid., pp. 249–50.
4. Theodore Draper, "How Not to Think about Nuclear War," *New York Review of Books*, 29, no. 12 (15 July, 1982). For critical comments by R. Peierls and others and Draper's replies, see ibid., no. 14 (23 Sept., 1982), pp. 58–61.

Index of Persons

Adam, 73, 80, 91, 113, 130
Allen, Ethan, 44
Altum, Bernard, 87–90, 95
Anselm, 7
Aquinas, Thomas, 11, 57, 78
Aristotle, 8, 14, 15, 43, 46, 54, 56, 66, 77, 78, 81, 104, 106
Augustine, 43
Austin, J. L., 19

Bach, J. S., 10
Berdyaev, Nicolas, 23, 27, 52, 58, 97, 98, 121, 135
Bergson, Henri, 8, 22, 23, 33, 61, 85, 105
Berlin, Isaiah, 19
Binet, Alfred, 61
Bradley, F. H., 31
Brutus, 26
Buddha, Gautama, 5, 6
Byron, G. N. G., 16

Caesar, Julius, 26, 33, 47, 48
Carnap, Rudolf, 104
Channing, W. E., vii
Cobb, J. B., 108
Confucius, 5
Crane, Stephen, 121
Cuhlman, Oscar, 43

Dante, Alighieri, 32, 97
Darwin, Charles, 67–72 *passim*, 86f
Dewey, John, 16
Dobzhansky, Theodosius, 84
Draper, Theodore, 133, 136
Driesch, Hans, 78

Eddy, Mary Baker, 5, 114
Edwards, Jonathan, 19
Einstein, Albert, vi, 71
Eisenhower, D. D., 132
Emerson, R. Waldo, 29, 44, 57, 72–73, 95
Epicurus, 15
Eve, 73, 115

Fechner, G. T., 27, 28, 73, 122, 135
Fitzgerald, Edward, 18
Franklin, Benjamin, 44
Freud, Sigmund, 37, 94, 126, 129
Friedman, Milton and Rose, 76

Gardner, Dr., 65
Garvie, A. E., 27
Gibbs, Willard, 69
Goethe, J. W., 86, 133
Goswami, Sri Jiva, 108

Hartshorne, The Rev. F. C., 73
Hartshorne, M. H., 124–125, 126
Heidegger, Martin, 36
Heraclitus, 8
Howard, Eliot, 88
Hugo, Victor, 124
Hume, David, 55, 104, 105, 109

Ikhnaton, 15, 125
Iqbal, 109
Isaiah, 14

James, William, 16, 44, 104
Jefferson, Thomas, 44
Jesus, 4, 60, 100–101, 106, 125
Job, 4, 32, 74, 75–76, 80

Subject Index

Abortion, 100, 103; *see* fetus, identity, person, pro-life, pro-personal life

Absolute and relative, God as, 44; *see* transcendence

Abstract, 9, 38; real in concrete, 46; God as, 9, 45f.; *see* concrete, eternal, necessary, primordial

Active and passive, *see* transcendence

Actual and potential, 10

Actuality, divine, 45, 77; of past, 33f.

Adaptation, presupposes order, 71; *see* laws

Aim, rational, 122f.; *see* reason

All-knowing, 27

All-powerful, 26

Altruism, explains self-interest, 108

Amerindians, 125

Analects, 114

Analogies, 30, 74; for God, 6, 21, 54–58, 81, 109; *see* anthropomorphism, mind-body, parent-child, relations, soul, World Soul

Animals, as not acting, 89; wisdom of, 91, 93; *see* instinct

Anthropomorphism, 28–30

Apes, 76

Arguments for theism, 117

Arms, nuclear, 131–33

Atheism, 7

Atomism, 8

Atoms, 8, 13, 30

Beauty, no greatest possible, 10; divine, 14; of love, 14; of world, 9, 25; *see* God, science, value

Becoming, 24; as reality itself, 8; as creative, 8, 77; rationale of, 10; *see* beauty, contingency, happiness, perfection

Behavior, species-destructive, 85

Being, as abstraction from becoming, 8, 24, 77

Bhagavad Gita, 40, 114

Bible, the, 2, 3; idolatrous views of, 67, 72f., 92, 114, 125; writers of, 91–92

Biblical view, the, 75

Big Bang, the, 49, 135

Biology, 30, 65, 66, 116

Birds, fossils of, 87; geographical distribution of, 90; primitive musical sense of, 89; songs of, 88f.

Birth: control, 102; experience, 128; rate, 92; *see* feminism

Body, divine right to rule one's, 60; God as having, 52, 54–56, 59, 133; as society, 58; *see* World Soul

Brains, 55, 113; more than thinking machines, 92

Buddhism, Buddhists, 108, 109

Calvinism, 72

Careers, human: 47, 117; begin and end, 35; finitude of essential, 35, 36; indestructible, 34f.; *see* immortality

Causa sui, 17; *see* self-creative

Cell theory of reality, 79

Related Titles From SUNY Press

CREATIVITY IN AMERICAN PHILOSOPHY. Charles Hartshorne.

INSIGHTS AND OVERSIGHTS OF THE GREAT THINKERS: An Evaluation of Western Philosophy. Charles Hartshorne.

THE SPIRIT OF AMERICAN PHILOSOPHY: A Revised Edition. John E. Smith.

HEGEL'S CONCEPT OF GOD. Quentin Lauer, S.J.

THE CHRISTOLOGY OF HEGEL. James Yerkes.

RECONSTRUCTION OF THINKING. Robert C. Neville.

BUDDHISM AND AMERICAN THINKERS. Kenneth K. Inada and Nolan P. Jacobson, Editors.

PERSPECTIVE IN WHITEHEAD'S METAPHYSICS. Steven David Ross.

THE EPOCHAL NATURE OF PROCESS IN WHITEHEAD'S METAPHYSICS. F. Bradford Wallack.

WHITEHEAD'S ORGANIC PHILOSOPHY OF SCIENCE. Ann Plamondon.

WHITEHEAD'S ONTOLOGY. John W. Lango.